LOST
MILL TOWNS OF
NORTH GEORGIA

LOST
MILL TOWNS OF
NORTH GEORGIA

Lisa M. Russell

THE
History
PRESS

Published by The History Press
Charleston, SC
www.historypress.com

First published 2020

Manufactured in the United States

ISBN 9781467143516

Library of Congress Control Number: 2019956058

For Louisa Russell.

May you learn the value of words and of hard work.

"I like good strong words that mean something…"

"Work is and always has been my salvation and I thank the Lord for it."

—*Louisa May Alcott,* Little Women

Contents

PREFACE

She haunts me. Her image hangs on my office wall. She is playing in the snow with her husband in Yorkship Village, New Jersey. She is the grandmother I never knew, but with all my heart I wish I had. The first time I saw this picture of Christina Moser, I recognized her, but we have never met. The Depression-era photo found its way to me years after she died. Gone without explanation.

I long to hear her advice. I wish my father hadn't hidden her from me. I have had to imagine what she was like and pretend I hear her voice. I can only imagine what she would say to me. I wonder, "Am I like her in any way?" I don't look like her, but I could have her personality. I wonder if she had my sardonic ways or if she was wiser than I, slower to speak and quick to listen. Sometimes I imagine she is whispering in my ear.

I have lived longer than my grandmother. She died in her forties and worked hard raising her family and supporting her husband. Christina and Louis Moser lived in a company town called Yorkship. This village was in Camden, New Jersey, and home to the New York Shipyards. The shipyards built many of the warships for both world wars. My grandfather was a welder and worked on battleships until his death in 1939. Three years later, my grandmother died, leaving my father an eight-year-old orphan.

Their death certificates were unclear—mesothelioma was an unknown. It is likely they both died from work-based asbestos. Shipbuilders used asbestos in the manufacturing process. The wives washed the infested clothes. By the time scientists uncovered this killer, the New York Shipyard had closed. Later, a fire destroyed all the records. I cannot prove it, but Louis died of asbestos poisoning, and Chrissy died of secondhand exposure. Until their deaths, they lived good upper middle-class lives in the shipyard village.

I always thought my father lived in a poor neighborhood. This conclusion came from the current state of Yorkship Village (now called Fairview). Looking past the current decay, Yorkship Village was built by the best industrial architects at the turn of the century in Camden, New Jersey. New York Shipyard built a modern and well-designed village for the workers.

A distant cousin clarified my view of what life was like for my father as a boy, before his parents died. Louis Moser was a skilled laborer. Along with his shipyard job, he worked on the Walt Whitman Bridge throwing rivets. He was good at many jobs in the shipyard, and he earned a good wage for his family.

My father never talked about his parents. Maybe it was too painful, or maybe he did not remember. I never asked, and I mourn what I did not know. The one thing I know is that he inherited his parents' tenacious work ethic—the same one he gave to me. With this legacy, I write this book. I write to praise the hardworking North Georgia millworkers who lived and worked in my adopted home state

Christine and Louis Moser. *Jenn Keller Clow.*

My father always worked in manufacturing. That brought me to North Georgia. My father moved us to Dalton, Georgia—the "Carpet Capital of the World"—in the late 1970s. We were about to make a life-changing move from Western New York to North Georgia.

Many years later, North Georgia is still my home. I write about this place so rich in history. I have written about the lost towns and the underwater towns. Now my legacy forced me somewhere else. The textile mills, some crumbling and other repurposed studio lofts, are fascinating. The textile timeline eclipses an era when hard work was valued. I feel an affinity to this historic time and these industrial places.

Hard work is in my DNA. I have a low tolerance for status quo and lackadaisicalness. I know where I get that. That is why I connected with the textile era—a time when people had to work and make a way or they did not survive. My ancestors had to work hard. Discovering this made me appreciate my own ethic. Finding Louis and Christina Moser, my blue-collar grandparents, has infused my life with a purpose. My purpose is to find and tell these lost stories of hardworking men, women and even children of the mills of North Georgia. I hope you enjoy them.

Acknowledgements

Every time I speak to groups about my books, I hope to leave this message: "Do not let your story die with you." Everyone has a story to tell and leave behind for their descendants. As writers, we want to steal them and send them forward. I am most thankful for those who left behind their voices to tell this story about the lost mill villages. If not for the oral histories in audio and video, their silence would make for a dull story.

Thank you to my dear friend and kindred spirit Dr. Donna Coffey-Little. Dr. Mary Lou Odom, your voice is with me as I write and try to find my own. On the opposite extreme, I thank those nameless English teachers I had in high school and as an undergraduate. Thank you for telling me in a hundred red marks and comments that I could never be a writer. You made me the English teacher I wish I had. And guess what? I am a writer.

To my biological sister, Ellen, who is always there cheering me on—thank you. To my spiritual sister, Ella—there is no one who can talk me down and point me to Daddy like you do. Ella, you always knew this would happen, but you let me figure it out for myself.

To my daughters-in-law, Becka and Laura Leigh, you have given me precious granddaughters—my gratitude is immeasurable. Becka, your help at GPB and other events has been appreciated. Laura Leigh, you're a great editor, and I thank you for the time it took for you to help me with this. To my sons who are fathers, Mike and John, take care of all my favorite girls: Charlotte, Josie and Louisa. John, thank you for sharing your research that introduced us to your great-grandmother and father. Mike, you remind me of my father. You are a hardworking man who takes good care of his family. And to my baby boy, Samuel K. Russell, I am proud of all you are and all that is coming your way. And to David, my husband of thirtysomething years—thank you for your support in this writing thing. My prayer is that all of you experience an awesome and intimate relationship with God for the rest of your days.

To my father, Donald Moser, who taught me the meaning of hard work and how to find fulfillment in a job well done. I thought of you often as I wrote about textile manufacturing. He was in the plastic industry in the early years of bread bags; he tweaked and even invented some early machines. He moved us to Dalton, Georgia, the "Carpet Capital of the World." I was not a happy teen about the move. He wrote me letters while I was still in Buffalo and tried to convince me that North Georgia was "God's country." He was right. God was there, and I met Him in "God's country" and that made all the difference.

To Jehovah Sabaoth, my Father-God, who meets me at the end of my rope and showed me how to tie a knot and hold on. Your peace overwhelms me as I get older, and your grace holds me when I doubt, fear and struggle with myself. I love you with all my heart.

IN APPRECIATION
Bartow County History Museum
Trey Gaines, director
Etowah Valley Historical Society
Joe Head
Whitfield-Murray Historical Society
Tina Pankey
Cherokee County Historical Society
Stefanie Joyner, executive director
Chieftains Museum, Rome
Heather Shores
Hargrett Rare Book & Manuscript Library, University of Georgia

CONTRIBUTORS
Barry Wright III
Dr. Donna Coffey-Little
Dr. Heidi Popham
Eleanor Hicks Popham and family
Beth Gibbons and family
Don Hayes
Wanda Kidd

INDIE BOOKSTORES AND MERCHANTS
Ken Studdard at Dogwood Books, Rome, GA
Carol Robson, General Mercantile and Café, Adairsville, GA
Macie Rittenhouse, Cabin Cuts, Canton, GA
The Southern Cove, Buddy and Jayson Fredrick, Cartersville, GA

Introduction

I hear them. And I want you to hear them too. We ignore them or just half-listen to their stories. We drive by their homes in the mill villages before decay has hidden its history. If you stop long enough, you might notice them. Repurpose or decay hides the mill village towns of North Georgia. Drive along and you might see a lonely stack or two, and down the road you look into the past. You might see a neat row of similar yet dissimilar homes still teeming with life next to a long-abandoned textile mill. A heavy pall surrounds the mill towns of North Georgia because the southern textile mill is dead.

The textile mill era, with accompanying mill villages, is over. What started in the late nineteenth century slowly dissipated after World War II, ending before the twenty-first century. The communities built around the company have disappeared. No longer does the local manufacturer supply and maintain low-rent housing, medical facilities, sporting events and a company store. For a time, paternalism made sense, but the world changed. The southern "Daddy" had to let the children go.

Chapter 1 tells the story of the textile mill era in North Georgia. This summary is the big picture, the puzzle all put together. The other chapters are the puzzle pieces. This is a micro-focus on each county with mill villages.

The mill towns included in this book had to meet specific criteria. It would have been impossible to include every mill in North Georgia in this book. The focus is the mills with accompanying towns. In most cases, the town and the mill are one entity. Some mill villages remain silent because the records could not be found.

Fulton and Greene Counties were originally included here but were removed for space reasons and because they were different that the mills in the true North Georgia area. I placed some of these chapters on my website, along with interactive maps of the mill locations (www.lisamrussell.net).

The South came to the Industrial Revolution party a little late, but North Georgia mills worked hard and contributed to industrial growth. When it was quitting time, and the silent whistle blew, the worker went home to start something new. Instead of allowing the mills to melt into the ground and disappear, some are creating new spaces from the rusty past and fading paint of old mill buildings.

The past is calling out to us. The millworkers want to tell their stories. They have so much to say. They can teach us about perseverance and struggle. We learn that management lost that fatherly feeling to stretch and wring out their laborers until they cried out. Can you hear them?

I can hear them. Listen. They punctuate their southern accents with mispronunciations and colloquialisms. What some would call uneducated, I call North Georgia culture—I respect that. Hear the stories of hardship. The North Georgia farmers and sharecroppers went to the mills for a steady paycheck. They were weary of the hardscrabble farm living.

Listen to the children speaking in the images of a social photographer. Early photographs gave voice to the little ones working in the dangerous mills—sad stories of children working as young as eight to add pennies to the family till.

Cheer for the local teams of the Southern Textile League, supported by most of the mills in North Georgia. A baseball game on a Saturday afternoon generated community and goodwill. All the single ladies dressed in their best, with their eyes on the prize of a textile ballplayer.

Notice the sounds of silence. The *clackety-clack* stops as the mill shuts down in the midst of union strikes. At some mills, you will hear gunshots in the uprising of 1934. You hear a governor's command call out the National Guard to quiet the uprising. They go unheard and back to work. They lost, but paternalism crumbles nonetheless, and the community of the mill villages fades away.

As the world changed in the 1960s, so did the textile industry. The shaky world of mill paternalism fell apart, and mill owners dumped the villages as world economies shifted. Textiles could be made cheaper somewhere else. The door slammed on the southern cotton industries, and the industry outsourced their legacy to other countries.

INTRODUCTION

My purpose is simple. I want to tell the story of this unique period in the voices of the people who lived and worked in the textile mills of North Georgia. The backstory is important, but the microphone is open to hear the mill people themselves.

For more stories, podcasts and interactive maps, please visit my website at www.lisamrussell. net and https://www.facebook.com/LostTowns.

CHAPTER 1

The Mill Village Era

THE SHIFT FROM AGRICULTURE TO INDUSTRY

North Georgia native and southern journalist Henry W. Grady was invited to speak, but he didn't want to. The New England Society of New York City had invited him. The members selected him because they had read his columns that were informed, conservative and industry friendly. On December 22, 1886, in the crowded Delmonico's restaurant, Grady was on the roster to speak, but not until General William Tecumseh Sherman had his say at the podium. Just after he finished, the band played "Marching through Georgia." The antagonistic mood was set for Henry Grady to talk about "The New South."

Grady began with a quote: "There was a South of slavery and succession—that South is dead. There is a South of Union and freedom—that South, thank God, is living, breathing, growing every hour." Grady quoted Benjamin H. Hill at Tammany Hall in 1866 and went on to describe the South in Reconstruction. He used vivid images of the Northern soldier and the Southern soldier returning home. One comes home to plenty of work and a home they remember, and the other comes home to poverty and destroyed homes. Grady shared the attitude of most defeated Southerners when he quoted Georgia author Bill Arp: "Well, I killed as many of them as they did of me and now, I'm going to work."

First American Cotton Mills in Pawtucket, Rhode Island. The original portion of the Slater Mills was built in 1793, and Cotton Production continued until 1895. *Library of Congress.*

Grady noted, "There is a new south, not through protest against the old, but because of new conditions, new adjustments and if you please, new ideas and aspirations." He pointed out that the southern cotton crop brought in $400 million annually and noted that if the people produced textiles near the crop, they would get rich. He reminded them of dropped interest rates for industry, from 24 to 6 percent. Grady told the northern industrialists that the path was smooth and the Mason-Dixon line erased. He did mention the "negro problem," but assured them that it was under control (an overestimation on Grady's part).

After his thirty-minute speech, he was welcomed with cheers and applause. In the audience of more than three hundred were big-name industrialists Henry Flagler and J.P. Morgan. The cotton mills were moving south, bringing the mills to the cotton fields. The time was ripe. While there had been cotton mills before the Civil War, the era of the textile mill in the South had begun.

Only a few textile mills operated in North Georgia before 1880. Trion, Roswell and New Manchester were running and had company-sponsored housing. By the late 1910s and early 1920s, the South was outproducing New England. The mills had moved south, just as Henry Grady suggested in his 1886 speech. The area called the Southern Piedmont stretched from Virginia to Alabama. Mills popped up in large urban areas and in small towns like Rome, Dalton, Cartersville, Calhoun and Trion. By the 1920s, textile mills had become the largest employers in North Georgia.

The allure of regular wages was too strong for farmers working on failing land. Images of North Georgia in the early twentieth century were of black-and-white canyons, from the erosion of topsoil. According to Stanley W. Trimble of the University of California, "Nearly 10 million acres were in cultivated row crops, and much of that land was losing soil in every rain. The Piedmont lost an average of about seven inches of its topsoil, but in many places all of it was lost. The resulting red hills were both the evidence and the heritage of generations of land mismanagement." The land was ruined for farming.

When land was cheap and unlimited in North Georgia (after the land lottery practically gave away the land that belonged to the Native Americans), the land was treated as expendable. Plantation owners, small farm owners and then sharecroppers raped the land. Trimble added:

Plantation owners viewed land as a tool to be used and discarded or laid by. Sharecroppers, like plantation owners, regarded land in the same way they viewed plows and mules—as an expendable tool for making a crop. The… sharecroppers did not own the land they worked and seldom stayed longer than one or two years on a farm. Sharecropper agriculture was a persistent enemy of the land because it was such an enduring and widespread practice.[1]

"Georgia cracker types."
Three bust-length studies of
North Georgia Mills workers
as interpreted by artist E.W.
Kemble (Edward Windsor),
1861–1933, pen and ink
on Bristol paper, February
1891. *Library of Congress.*

The land was in disrepair, and farmers looked elsewhere for income. At the same time, textile mills were flush with new technologies that increased production. They needed new hands to work the new machinery. So, the North Georgia mills lured families from the farm with low-rent homes with modern upgrades like water near the house. Later, indoor plumbing and electricity were added, all for the low price of twenty-five cents per room per week. The entire family was expected to work in the mill—even the children.

Merchants also tightened credit in the late 1800s, making it impossible for the economically distressed farmers to get out of their red-clay and financial holes. Some blamed it on the boll weevil. Georgia author William Rawlings said that is a myth: "The popular myth holds that cotton production, which had so richly rewarded Georgia's agriculture-based economy for more than a century, was irreparably damaged by the arrival of the boll weevil."[2] Historians of the era know that there were other factors that crashed the cotton crop, forcing more farmers into mill villages in the early 1920s. World War I and a recession in 1920–21 caused cotton prices to fall.[3]

This was the beginning of paternalism. Some scholars compare paternalism in the textile mills to the slave/master relationship, but that metaphor does not truly work in this situation. Paternalism was a system that allowed the mill owners to attract failing farmers and poor southerners by offering them a home and a community as part of the job. Paternalism had a downside, like children millworkers and a "big brother" control over workers at home. Eventually, paternalism crumbled. Douglas Flamming noted that the paternalistic system was weak, without a foundation and would fall apart under certain conditions. Those conditions happened.[4]

When the mill operators decided to introduce production science, they created the dreaded "stretch-out" system. Workers were let go, and the remaining operatives had to run more machines at a faster pace. The family system started to break down. By the early 1920s, labor unions had started to move south and focus on textile mills.

Whole families worked in the mill because one wage earner was not enough. In the early 1900s, children as young as eight worked in the mills. The younger children did their part by dressing up in their Sunday best and selling lunch baskets to the other workers at noon. According to researchers at Georgia State University, "Between 1880 and 1910, roughly a quarter of all textile workers were under the age of 16." Social reformers like photographer Lewis W. Hine and the National Child Labor Committee (NCLC) worked hard to stop the practice, but it continued until New Deal laws ended it. However, the GSU researchers reported, "Children did not disappear from the mills in the South until economic conditions and technological advancements made their labor more expensive than that of adults."[5] Life in the mill was different than life on the farm.

Families worked together on the farm and for long hours—having their children work alongside of them was nothing new. Working long hours was not new to these farmers either, but at least they could control the work pace and conditions. The mills were noisy and hot. Lint flew in the air, covering everything and everybody. The machinery was dusted, but the operatives carried it on their clothes and in their lungs. The work was monotonous and toilsome. A worker compared the farm to the mill: "In farming, you do work real close to nature. There's always something exciting and changing in nature." Change was coming to paternalism as well.

Everything began to fall apart when the millworkers started raising their voices to their "Daddies." The mill owners were not holding up their end. They were making workers labor harder for less. They were exercising too much control over the workers' lives. Unions began to form.

In 1900, more than 90 percent of millworkers lived in mill towns. The owners built churches and insisted the workers attend. They started free schools, but many of their workers could not attend due to working in the mills. They had a police force that kept workers from drinking and going outside the mills for entertainment. The workers were not getting ahead as

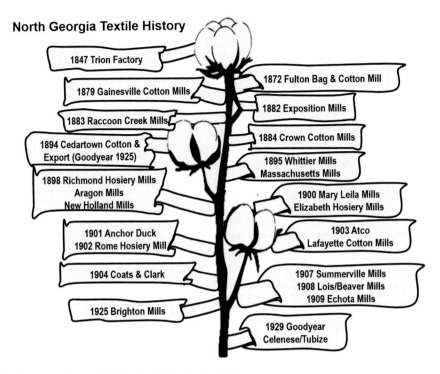

The cotton mills of North Georgia. *Author's collection.*

they once thought they might after leaving the farm. They were worse off and less healthy.

Workers were spied on in some mills and reported if they talked about unions. Yet the workers still met in secret and decided to sign union cards. The General Textile Strike of 1934 was sometimes violent, and the Georgia National Guard was called out during this widespread revolt. The strike was unsuccessful and, in some cases, tragic, but more strikes changed the relationship between worker and owner.

African Americans are included in this book, but their part is small. A lasting and sad legacy of Reconstruction in the South was not only segregation in the mills but also the total exclusion of African Americans. Southern textile mills were mostly for "whites only." Black laborers did work in the mill, but only doing the worst jobs like emptying the "Dookey Wagon" or moving bales of cotton at rock-bottom pay. African American women did not work in the early mills at all. They found jobs caring for kids and keeping house for the workers.[6]

PATERNALISM: DADDY'S TAKIN' CARE OF YOU SO GOOD!

From the beginning, "Father" knew best. An unusual relationship between mill owner and millworker existed during the textile era. As early as the antebellum mills, owners wanted to provide for their operatives like parents provide for children. Social scientists have given this practice the term "paternalism." The definition is wide ranging, but for the purpose of this story, paternalism is when a mill takes care of its own. Some have compared this to the master and slave relationship, the mill being the plantation, but this analogy is extreme.

The operatives had a choice to leave the farm and join the mill village. The workers, although it was a bare living wage at first, were paid. The provision of homes, stores, recreation and education were not in place of pay. Pay was a source of strife between workers and owners—this led to strikes and attempts at unionization. Workers were paid so low that the entire family had to work, including young children.

"Daddy" had an ulterior motive. He needed reliable laborers. Providing recreation kept them home and sober. Most villages prohibited liquor and the making of spirits. Workers only had one and a half days off. Managers wanted to make sure they had something to do and somewhere to go. The

This home still exists at 210 Park Avenue, Lindale, Georgia. This was Norman Hall's home in 1913. Note the tall northern-style roof, which were needed up north for snow removal. Later, homes were modified for cost and the lack of snow. *Author's collection.*

main thing was to keep them working for as cheap as they could pay these former farmers.

"Management wanted the workers to be in churches because they felt the churches domesticated the workers," said Father George Kloster, from a former mill area in Gastonia, North Carolina. He continued, "[Churches] would keep them from getting too uppity, and so that's why there seemed to be a hand-in-glove relationship between the management and many of the churches."[7] Churches were often built and managed by the mill. Daddy was taking care of everything.

In *The Uprising of '34*, a documentary about the General Textile Strike of 1934, the narration is provided by the people who lived during the strike. One worker remembered what management said during the strike: "We had a job for 'em if they wanted it. If they didn't, all they had to do is go back to the hills."

Another worker commented, "People was too darn sorry to pay anybody enough to live on because they're afraid to go and get a little bit ahead, then they can't get 'em to work for nothin'." He continued, "Like a man told me up in North Georgia, 'Keep a man hungry, and he'll work,' that's the truth."[8]

DESIGNER TOWNS AND VILLAGES

No two mill villages in North Georgia were the same. Some mill homes were nothing more than boarded shacks. Others were well-designed brick homes that endure a century later. The early homes boasted of water nearby but had no indoor plumbing or electricity. Later villages like Celanese near Rome, built in the late 1920s, boasted of floorplan choice and indoor plumbing. Most added the indoor plumbing and electricity, but villages like Crown Mill only allowed one bulb for the entire house and charged for that.

The living conditions that many children of the Rome Hosiery Mill lived under were not much better than their working conditions. The configuration of the mill villages could be described as more like slave quarters than of sharecroppers' accommodations. The average home at the mill consisted of a run-down house that was often put together very crudely. There was also very little privacy since the houses were so close together.[9]

Chicopee in Hall County was built by Johnson & Johnson. The company employed a community designer to place the homes on winding roads with

The village included services such as a school, a clinic, a general store, a pharmacy and several fire houses. Residents remember this building having a soda fountain. It now serves as a haunted location during Halloween. Tubize (Celanese), Rome, Georgia, 2019. *Author's collection.*

The mill did not intend on building a village when it opened, as it had gone out of fashion, but the mill owners had to have a place for their workers to live. All the houses were built of brick. Workers could choose from five different home plans, including single-family homes of three to six rooms and efficiency duplexes. All the homes came with indoor plumbing and electricity. Tubize (Celanese), Rome, Georgia, 2019 *Author's collection.*

various floorplans. Chicopee, as part of the Johnson & Johnson mission, was ruled by sanitary lifestyles. A guidebook listed the rules for living in the village homes:

> *HOUSEHOLD REGULATIONS:*
> *Keep wash basins, bath tubs and water closet clean. (Special brushes are provided for this purpose.)*
> *Keep your cook stoves and ice boxes clean.*
> *Keep walls and ceilings clean in every room.*
> *Keep porches clean.*
> *Keep screens in windows through the summer.*
> *Report at once any trouble with the lights or plumbing.*
> *Keep grass on lawns cut, and ground around house clean and free from rubbish.*
> *Do not allow garbage or ashes to collect upon the premises. Put them in the cans provided for this purpose.*
> *These cans will be collected, and their contents disposed of daily without charge.*
> *Do not waste water and electric current. Turn off all electric lights, water faucets and electric stoves or heaters as soon as you are through with them.*
> *Follow all directions of visiting nurse when she makes her regular inspections of the premises.*[10]

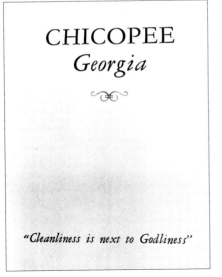

Chicopee Village Manual. Notice the focus on sanitary living. The author photographed the manual at the Hargrett Archives at the University of Georgia.

Lindale's homes were photographed by Lewis Hine. One caption stated that nothing was spared in the building of these homes except the children, meaning that more care was put into building quality houses than providing a safe home for children to live outside the mill. Other Rome mill homes were not as well designed.

Homes for Rome Hosiery and Anchor Duck were later condemned and demolished. Celanese brick homes and Lindale's solid structures are lived in today. Other villages like Atco in Cartersville, Canton Mills and Echota in Calhoun have homes in various stages of decay and rescue. While some real estate companies came in to repurpose the mills into lofts, shopping and office space, the homes were left to individuals to rejuvenate the dwellings.

The mill village era was isolated in a time frame that depended on the textile mills' growth from the late 1800s all the way until the 1950s and 1960s. Although the companies sold off the mill bungalows, some communities remained without the paternalistic support. Reunions are evidence that the dwellings were more than houses provided by the mills—they were homes.

MILL FLOOR

The mill floor was a noisy, busy and dangerous place. Ubiquitous stories fly around about the lint that got onto clothes and into lungs. The mill was dangerous in so many ways. When children worked in the mills, they would climb on machines to change spindles and could fall into the machines. Constantly moving machines could catch loose limbs and clothing. The noise was deafening and disorienting. The windows were often shut or painted black.

People chewed tobacco and spit in the corner and in the heads of the machines where the gears were. They started painting the corners white so you could see where they were spitting. A twelve-hour shift would end in filthy clothes and bodies. In one mill, a smoking area was open with red benches. In the 1970s, they would even smoke marijuana on the benches.

One mill owner wanted workers to ration their toilet paper to save money. Mattie Rainwater Whatley remembered:

And boss said we had to be savin' with the toilet paper...and not using it more than we had to. And they told us if they caught us wasting the paper, they was gonna lay us off. So, I got me a corn cob at the house, carried it

*over to the plant, and we tied the string around it, and drove a nailed up
at the back of the commode, and put a sign, big sign, "Use this cob, and
save your job."*

*And the boss said if he ever found out who did that, he was gonna fire
'em. And I was scared to death.*[11]

Shannon Mill had troughs of oil flowing through it, according to a former employee, Wanda Kidd. She had to stop working in the section of the mill with the oil as it caused her to break out. She remembered having to blow into a tube to test for brown lung.[12]

Missing from the mill floor in the early years of the textile era were African Americans. Black men could not work on the mill floor, and women were not hired at all. They could work in the warehouse, but they were never allowed to run machines. They were saving those jobs for the whites.

Black women worked for the millworkers in their homes. They watched their children while their white mothers worked in the mill. They didn't have to pay them very much. They managed the white millworkers' homes and raised their children. Grace Gardin Wilson remembered:

*You could take your black hands and you could stir their dough, hands in
their foods, and you could take your black body and lay in the bed with the
child, protectin' them. But you couldn't come in their front door, right? You
weren't worthy to come in their front door.*[13]

The white millworkers were poor, but they hired black women because they were the only ones not able to get a mill job—these woman had nowhere else to work. The African American men had only certain jobs they could do in the mill. One worker remembered in a North Georgia mill seeing a segregation era remnant: a metal dispenser full of paper cone cups hung on the wall above the water fountain. There was no need for a sign—the workers who worked there before the 1970s knew that it was a black-only water fountain.

TOO YOUNG TO WORK

Lewis Hine's photographs changed the world. When Hine came to North Georgia for the National Child Labor Committee, he took pictures of children, the least of these in our society. The images were given to the U.S. Congress and changed labor laws.

Lewis W. Hine traveled fifty thousand miles every year for the National Child Labor Committee. Hine used his images to "awaken the consciousness of the nation, and change the reality of life for millions of impoverished, undereducated children."[14]

Group of workers in a Georgia hosiery mill, April 1913. Lewis Hine, photographer. *Library of Congress.*

Above: Lili Strainers, seven years old here, was the same age her mother was when she began working. Her mother said, "I ain't going to put her to work if I can help it. I'm going to give her as much education as I can so she can do better than I did." Atlanta, Georgia. Lewis Hine, photographer. *Library of Congress.*

Opposite, top: Photographer Lewis Hine reported, "Mrs. Dora Stainers, 562½ Decatur St. 39 years old. Began spinning in an Atlanta Mills at 7 years and is in this Mills work for 32 years. Only 4 days of schooling in her life. Began at 20 cents a day. The most she ever made was $1.75 a day & now she is earning $1 a day when she works. She is looking for a job." *Library of Congress.*

Opposite, middle: "Mrs. Stainers is a woman of exceptional ability considering her training," recorded photographer Lewis Hine. She attended four days of school. *Library of Congress.*

Opposite, bottom: Hines noted, "Another 'Dependent Father'...he made application for his minor children to work." And he worked part time. Although he was from south Georgia, this was also true of North Georgia in this period. Lewis Hine, photographer. *Library of Congress.*

Images of these children changed the minds of lawmakers. Laws were proposed in the 1900s, but it took the New Deal to enforce the laws that the states refused to implement. Hine, a New York schoolteacher, left his job to work for a nonprofit, using an outdated camera, preserving the era of child labor in pictures that spoke more than words.

Child labor in the mills started as a carry-over from children working on the farm. This culture just translated into the textile mill. Some mill owners required the entire family to work if they lived in their homes—in some reports from Hine and others, the father of the home would get his

A little spinner in a Georgia cotton mill, January 1909. Lewis Hine, photographer. *Library of Congress.*

entire family working in the mill and then would not work full time or would stop working completely. In Lindale, a store on Booze Mountain was the place many men would sit and drink all day while their families toiled away in the mill.

Rome Hosiery Mill had some of the worst working environments. Lewis Hine documented shoeless child workers in this mill. The floors were greasy, and the National Child Labor Committee member commented, "It seems that it would be easy for anyone to slip and fall against those rapidly moving spindles, wheels, cogs and belts and be injured—perhaps killed."[15]

Georgia was one of the last states to even acknowledge the child labor laws, in 1907. Real change did not happen until it was a federal law enacted in the mid-1930s. The mill owners tried every tactic to keep the children in the mills. Thomas Dawley, former investigator for the U.S. Bureau of Labor, was hired by the manufacturers to discredit the child labor reformers. He said children benefited from mill work, that it was good for their growth and improved their development. He stated that it helped children seek education, but the fact was that child workers never stayed in school and most had less than a fifth-grade education.

Right: Young spinners in Floyd Cotton Mills, Rome, Georgia, April 1913. Lewis Hine, photographer. *Library of Congress.*

Below: Photographer Lewis Hine said that all these workers were from the Rome Hosiery Mills. Two are eleven years old, and some are only nine or ten. The youngest earned about three dollars per week for turning, knitting or looping. The fifteen-year-old boys were making six to nine dollars per week "if they're speedy." Rome, Georgia. *Library of Congress.*

Little spinner girls in a Georgia mill. Lewis Hine, photographer. *Library of Congress.*

The mills provided a school, but they did not push education. Children attended school when they could. Most did not take advantage of it. Captain Meikleham from Lindale Mills told a labor investigator that he provided the schools and even night schools, but they did not go. Although most schools did have compulsory education laws, mills ignored them.[16]

Although a child labor reform bill was passed in Georgia in 1907, the laws were ignored. The New Deal reforms mandated that federal laws be enforced. Children soon disappeared from the mills. As technology improved, small children were used less. It cost the mills more money than the child laborer was worth.[17] Later, as the laws changed, the children filed out of the mills and into the schools.

Gainesville mill resident Herman Hooper felt like it was a good life. He remembered that they had indoor plumbing in the village, while others in Hall still used outhouses. Hooper remembered the school and the teachers were all supplied by the mill. Former mill village kids jokingly recalled, "Students had their own uniforms—a pair of overalls and a white shirt for the boys and plain cotton dresses for the girls." Another resident chimed in, "It wasn't required; it was all we had."[18] Gainesville Mill's school burned to the ground in the village in 1973. Children of the mills in the earlier days did not have it as good as Mr. Hooper.

Above: Doffer boys in a Georgia cotton mill. Lewis Hine, photographer. *Library of Congress.*

Left: Norman Hall, born on October 1, 1901, lived at 210 Park Street in Lindale, Georgia. He worked at Massachusetts Mills as a doffer at ten and a half years old. Lewis Hine, photographer. *Library of Congress.*

Lindale homes remarked on by Hine: "Nothing was neglected, but the child." Hine felt the homes were well constructed and modern, but the children of the looms were not treated properly. This is the reason he traveled throughout the South and photographed children in dangerous mills. *Library of Congress.*

Norman Hall, a child laborer in Lindale in the early 1900s, was not able to go to school and never learned to write. His military record during World War II shows he had to sign his name with an "X." He moved from mill to mill because he could not move up without an education. Looking at his picture, he looks older than his ten years. Mill life may have destroyed his health, but the greatest loss was a childhood.

MILL VILLAGE LIFE: FROM BASEBALL TO BEANS

Baseball was a big deal in the textile era. Almost every mill village in North Georgia had a baseball team. This was not amateur play—many of these mill villagers went to play in the big leagues. The players were serious, and mill owners recruited players just to play rather than work. Or they hired players to do easy jobs like village painting so they would be fresh on game day. The competition was fierce, especially in the Northwest Georgia Textile League.

Shannon managers wanted to donate part of their wages to recruit Rudy York from Atco. "Lefty" Sproull played for Goodyear in Rockmart, but he spent many seasons moving around the Southeast playing. He was hard to get a hit off, according to his granddaughter Beth Gibbons.[19]

The company constructed recreation areas and sponsored activities like basketball, bowling and scouting, but baseball was the big deal in the mill villages. The mill owners built the baseball fields and added lights, creating

Anchor Duck Mills textile baseball team. *Front row, left to right*: Frank Kearce, unknown, Ted Ammons, A.S. "Red" Scott, Charlie Padget and "Left" Hutchings. *Back row, left to right*: unknown, Claude Shumate, Virgil Jefts, Robby Whitt, Luke Gravely, Bobby Adams, Russ Lyons, Kewt Kearce and unknown. The identity of the young boy sitting up front is unknown. *Rome History Museum.*

Early Atco Mills baseball team in Cartersville, Georgia. *Bartow History Museum.*

a mill village event each Saturday after work. The mill owners supported textile baseball by recruiting and catering to the ballplayers. The players were given "jobs" in the mill, but their real purpose was to win ballgames.

Why did the mills invest so much in their baseball teams? According to historian Heather Shores, many scholars felt that management wanted to promote teamwork, keep the worker's busy and avoid unionization. Others felt it was all about the players learning about mill life—especially immigrants and former farmers. It may just have been another way to keep players in the village by paying them extra wages. During the Great Depression, players made twelve to fourteen dollars per week for mill work and an extra four to seven dollars for playing. A higher salary tended to keep the player in the mill.[20]

Game day was a big event. Beth Gibbons noted, "My grandmother and her sisters wouldn't think of going to a game without dresses, hats and gloves. In that community, you only dated ballplayers."[21]

The rules changed a lot during league, but one rule was constant: every player had to be a mill employee, and the mill employee had to be white. African Americans had their own teams, and the two never mixed. Black

A "dirty" Atco (Goodyear) baseball team. Cartersville, Georgia. *Bartow History Museum.*

Rudy York (*left*) was a hometown hero for Atco's "Super Twisters" in the Northwest Georgia Textile League, an independent semipro league. York went on to play third base for the Detroit Tigers on opening day, 1937. *Bartow History Museum.*

workers did not even come to the white mill games. The textile mill era was still the segregationist South.

Many textile ballplayers went on to play professionally, but Atco had one of the greats. Each Saturday after the mill had closed for the week, the village went to the Atco baseball field and sat in the grandstand. The lucky ones were able to watch Rudy York.

The "Home Run King," Preston Rudolph "Rudy" York began his baseball career in 1929 at age fifteen on the ball fields of Atco. According to the Etowah Valley Historical Society, "The 'Super Twisters' were one of the founding members of the Northwest Georgia Textile League in 1931, an independent semi-pro league that included a number of teams from mill towns in the surrounding area, including those in Cedartown, Rockmart others around Rome, Georgia." He was so good that six supervisors at Brighton mill in Shannon pledged one dollar from their salaries each week to lure Rudy York to the Brighton team away from Atco.[22]

An early Textile League game in Atco, Georgia. *Bartow History Museum.*

Atco "Super Twisters," Carterville, Georgia. *Bartow History Museum.*

Canton Mills baseball team, 1938. *Cherokee Historical Society.*

Goodyear baseball in Atco, Georgia. *Bartow History Museum.*

James "Lefty" Sproull Jr. (1904–1975) is on the back row, second from the left. Lefty played for Goodyear Rockmart from 1935 to 1945. He also played in Huntsville, Alabama, before returning to Rockmart. *Beth Gibbons.*

In 1937, Rudy York was on the lineup as third baseman for the Detroit Tigers' opening day. He was benched during the season due to poor play but eventually moved to the catcher's spot so he could bat. According to Terry Sloope writing for the Society for American Baseball Research, "Rudy proceeded to break Babe Ruth's record of most home runs in a single calendar month by hitting eighteen home runs in August [a record he held until June 1998, when Sammy Sosa hit twenty home runs]."[23]

Rudy played for the Boston Red Sox, the Chicago White Sox and the Philadelphia Athletics. He had thirteen years in the major leagues, and while there, he patented the "Tracker" glove and held a *Ripley's Believe It Not!* record. He was written up for having broken two windows in the same car with two grand slams.[24]

He was released from the Athletics but stayed in the game by managing minor-league teams, coaching first base and even playing semipro ball. He died in 1970, and Governor Jimmy Carter declared August 17 to be "Rudy York Day" in Georgia.[25]

THE WINGFOOT CLAN

ATCO EDITION

PROTECT OUR GOOD NAME

VOL. 7   WEDNESDAY, NOVEMBER 24, 1937   No. 11.

Club Show is Well Attended

The November Employees Night Program, sponsored by the Woman's Club on last Saturday evening was greatly enjoyed by the small audience present.

The unusually cold wave was responsible for the small number attending.

A full hour of entertainment was furnished by Atco youngsters under the able direction of Mrs. Smith, music teacher and Miss Sanders, expression teacher.

The next program will be the Christmas pageant sponsored by the school. Date will be announced later.

Rev. Millsap Returns To Atco Church

It was announced by the North Georgia Methodist Conference, as the Clan goes to press, that Rev. S. H. Millsapp has been reappointed to the pastorate of the Atco Methodist Church for the coming year.

In view of the splendid record Rev. Millsap made last conference year, it was expected that he would be permitted to continue the good work.

The Clan joins in with his host of friends in wishing him continued success in the church.

P.-T. A.

The Atco Parent-Teachers' Association held its first meeting of the school year in the auditorium Friday, November 5, 1937. The meeting was called to order by the president, Mrs. Linderson and a very interesting play entitled "An Athletic Wedding," was presented by Miss Hill's fifth grade.

The business meeting was opened by singing the P.-T. A. song and repeating the Lord's Prayer. A report on the Pre-School clinic, held May 12 was given by Miss Gould.

Mrs. Linderson announced that meetings would be held on the first Friday of each month.

A count of mothers by grades was taken, Miss Vincent's 7th grade and Miss Fullis' first grade tied with ten each.

Home-coming Party Honoring Rudy York

One of the most enjoyable parties ever staged in Atco, was held at the Womans Club House on October 29, in honor of Rudy York. Invited were Rudy's old team mates, the boys he first played baseball with, back in the early years of '29, '30 and '31. Also, the present ball club and the overseers of the Mill were included.

In the above picture, in the foreground, Ed Sharpe, Rudy's first manager, is shown congratulating York on his outstanding success with the Detroit Tigers. Looking on are his former team-mates. Left to right as follows: Bobbie Dupree George Johnson, Henry Ray, Frank Cornet, Lovick West, Paul Pinton, Arthur Parker, Roy Henderson, Lloyd Looney, and K. C. Hudgins. (Missing was "Bunk" Morris, who couldn't be found when this picture was made.) A face that all of the team keenly missed was genial Bob Powell's, his place was taken by Arthur Parker.

In the left insert, the cameramen caught Rudy York and Joe Stearns in an amicable argument, with Jimmy Knight and

Guy Parmenter as interested spectators.

Decorating the room, preparing the food, and serving were handled capably by the Domestic Science Class of the school, pictured in the right insert, as ilows: Front row, left to right;

Christin Hartsfield, and Betty Catherine Ray, Myrom Golden. Jo McCoy. Back row: left to right; Nancy Ruth Ayers, Miss Jewel Gould, teacher, Miss Jimmie Wofford and Doris Wilder. The spirit of halloween was (Continued on page 2.)

Their Suggestions Paid Dividends

Left to right: John Middlebrooks, Joe Rowland, Deward Waldrep, and John Henry Sparks.

At the last meeting of the Suggestion Committee, it was found that suggestions submitted by the above group of employees were eligible for awards (Continued on page 2.)

Red Cross Drive Soon

The annual drive by the Red Cross for members and the money necessary to carry on their great work in times of need is now on all over the United States

However, due to the present running schedule of the Mill and the shut-down this week, only those employees who are working will be asked at this time to contribute.

Please remember this is a voluntary contribution, a n d when the call is made everyone should do his or her part in contributing to a most worthy cause.

Missionary News

The Methodist Missionary Society held its November meeting at the home of Mrs. W. H. Millsap, No. 5 Mayflower Street. Devotional service was given by Mrs. W. H. Millsap. Mrs. S. M. Millsap led the prayer.

New officers were elected as follows: Mrs. O. A. Farmer, president; Mrs. H. E. Duncan, vice-president; Mrs. Allie Soper, corresponding secretary; Mrs. Frances Harris, recording secretary; Mrs. W, H. Millsap, treasurer; Miss Grace Millsap, superintendent of baby specials; Miss Kathleen Duncan, superintendent of publicity; Mrs. Ethel Bearden, superintendent of (Continued on page 2.)

PREVENT FREEZING

Every night, when the thermometer is near the freezing point, take no chances, cut your water off. Water freezing in the plumbing system in your house can do a great deal of damage in bursted pipes, etc.

When you leave home over the week, salt should be placed in the commodes and lavatory to prevent freezing in the traps.

If anyone does not understand just how the cut off valves in your house works, see Mr. Stewart, Mr. Jones or the Labor Department.

The November 24, 1937 Atco edition of Wingfoot Clan, produced by Goodyear. The banner over the articles about blood drives, PTA, incentives, turning your water off when it freezes and Rudy York's return is the motto "Protect Our Good Name." *Bartow History Museum.*

At the Rome Braves Stadium, there is a monument to the textile leagues. Historian Heather Shores set up a series of posters telling about the players of the Northwest Georgia Textile League. She wrote, "During the years that the Northwest Georgia Textile League was active, the customs surrounding the players, the teams, and their fans served to unite the members of the Floyd County community and bolster the community spirit of the industrial families within the area."[26]

THE COMPANY STORE

Trion Mills had the "Big Friendly." Other mill villages just had the company store. Stores like Atco's were owned by outsiders but leased by the mill. Every village had a store nearby so they could purchase goods, mostly on company credit, to survive. Low wages required weekly loans on their pay; the mill issued blue books, company tokens and chips as ancient bitcoin against their pay. Millworkers remembered getting "NB" on their pay envelopes meaning they had nothing left after the company store was paid.

The old Earnest Tubbs sang, "I sold my soul to the company store." This explains what many villagers experienced. Workers got caught in a hole and had a hard time digging out of debt. Small pay envelopes got smaller.

Stores in self-contained mill villages allowed credit, but they charged more for the privilege. Most villagers did not have cars until after World War II, so trips to town were limited. The company store had a monopoly, and it charged more for goods.

Like most, the Gainesville mill village was self-contained. It had gardens all over the village and pens for cows and hogs. It had a school, a doctor, a store and even a theater on site. There was a downside. Everything was free or on credit. Rent and groceries were taken out of their pay. Longtime resident Boswell said, "There's a lot of people that worked in that mill and never drawed a dime—[the mill would] take all of their paycheck every week." Mill families were skilled at "making do." With little cash to spend, the company took care of them.

The company store was essential because people could not go to town without transportation. They paid for groceries with "chits" ripped from booklets provided by the mill instead of money. They could also draw on their next paycheck at the company store.

Some these stores still stand. Crown Mills had a mill store on the corner in the village, across from the mill. The building still stands and is waiting its new purpose courtesy of the City of Dalton. In Celanese, the mill store and pharmacy building remain in the Riverside district of Rome. The building is now covered with graffiti and serves as a haunted location at Halloween.

STRETCH-OUTS AND STRIKES: THE RELATIONSHIP IS OVER

Telling the textile mill era story requires an honest look at the many strikes that erupted. Each mill has its own version, but the general premise was that the paternalistic system broke down. The owners could no longer keep their promises of steady work. When there was work, the management applied the early century scientific approaches to production. They required workers to do more for the same pay. They were tortured by the men standing behind them with stopwatches. They were tired of the "stretch-outs" and layoffs due to overproduction.

So, the operatives rebelled against "Daddy" in the form of strikes. They were stirred up by the unions moving south, determined to sign up as many textile workers as they could. They brought in pickets and squadrons to promote their gospel of organized labor.

The strikes led to lost wages and production and even bloodshed. Governor Talmadge often interfered, calling out the Georgia National Guard, and he even put a group of striking women in a former World War I German POW camp in Atlanta.

The worst strike was the General Textile Strike of 1934. Gangs of union organizers came to many towns in North Georgia enticing workers to leave their looms and strike for better wages and treatment by the mills. Some towns followed; most did not.

Governor Eugene Talmadge declared martial law against protestors, and armed guardsmen loaded up and arrested these women during the 1934 textile strike. *Atlanta Journal-Constitution Photographic Archives, Special Collections and Archives, Georgia State University Library.*

National Guardsmen
round up protesting
textile workers, 1934.
From the Atlanta
Journal-Constitution.

The 1934 textile strike
made its way to Atco,
Georgia. *Bartow History
Museum.*

Striking textile workers
being escorted by
the National Guard
to a World War I
internment camp that
once held German
prisoners, 1934. Atlanta
Journal-Constitution
*Photographic Archives,
Special Collections and
Archives, Georgia State
University Library.*

National Guard transporting striking textile workers to a prisoner camp during the 1934 textile strike. Atlanta Journal-Constitution *Photographic Archives, Special Collections and Archives, Georgia State University Library.*

The '34 uprising. *Photographic Collection, 1920–1976, Special Collections and Archives, Georgia State University Library.*

Pickets outside Mary Leila Mills, Greensboro, Georgia, 1941. Jack Delano, photographer. *Library of Congress.*

Millworkers who lived largely in rural areas are here being taken through CIO picket line at a textile mill in Greensboro, Georgia. The lockout lasted about three months, ending in a signed contract. Mary Leila Mills, Greensboro. *Library of Congress.*

Greensboro chief of police reading CIO picket sign at Mary Leila Mills, Greensboro, Georgia, May 1941. Jack Delano, photographer. *Library of Congress.*

Pickets outside a textile mill at Mary Leila Mills, Greensboro, Georgia, 1941. Jack Delano, photographer. *Library of Congress.*

CIO pickets jeering at a few workers who were entering Mary Leila Mills, Greensboro, May 1941. Jack Delano, photographer. *Library of Congress.*

Chief of police talking to CIO pickets outside Mary Leila Mills, May 1941. *Library of Congress.*

The *Atlanta Constitution* reported, "An independent survey indicated approximately 48,000 employees had returned to work with 13,000 idle."[27] The paper also reported more than twenty days after the workers went on strike on September 3, many mills were back to work: "Officials announced that 122 of Georgia's 157 cotton mills were again in operation."[28]

The National Guard stayed on duty. Five companies of guardsmen with three to four hundred men were stationed throughout the state. Three companies remained in Shannon at Southern Brighton Mill. One other company remained on duty at Rockmart. According to the *Atlanta Constitution*, Adjutant General Lindley Camp said the troops would be kept at the ills until "we are certain that order has been restored."[29]

Hear the voices of the workers. Hear the shouts of the pickets who listened to the taunting of the "Flying Squadrons." Listen as families move from the mill villages when they were evicted, sold out or moved on. Strain your ears to hear the final whistles across the decades that marked the end of the textile era.

CHAPTER 2

BARTOW COUNTY

CARTERSVILLE

American Tire Company (Atco), 1904

His hands were shaking. His eyes darted around the room. This was not like Governor Joe Frank Harris. In 1988, he was accosted by the press, and he was angry. A newspaper article suggested that his Quality Basic Education Act would not be funded because of a budget shortage. He was passionate about this plan to improve education for all Georgia children. He called the report a lie and said he was not dismantling this plan "because it is a child of this administration and it was birthed in this administration."

Marietta Daily Journal reporter Andy Bowen interviewed Governor Harris in private after he noticed his strong reaction to this piece of legislation. Bowen asked, "Do you feel your own early education was adequate?" The governor had settled down and answered quietly, simply, "No."

Governor Harris explained why this issue was so personal: "Certainly. I think that we can always improve. I know in my own education, I had as good an education as could be offered during the period of time…but I realize that I've got shortcomings that maybe education might could have helped correct, that I struggle every day trying to deal with.…I came from the old Atco-Goodyear Cotton Mill Village, and my first five years was in the school there in that textile mill village. I think I can identify with a lot of the problems that students are having in the outlying areas out in the state."

Harris attended the Goodyear mill school in Cartersville because his father was an employee until 1945. The American Textile Company built a textile mill and village in 1904 north of Cartersville. The mill operated the school, but in 1929, it collaborated with Bartow County schools. Funding came from the mill and the State of Georgia teacher salaries. On December 2, 1957, Cartersville annexed Atco as part of the city. Harris transferred to Cartersville High School his senior year. The Atco school closed six years later in 1963.[30]

While Harris felt that he missed the basics and needed help with algebra, his other grades made up for it. Emory University offered Harris a scholarship. He ended up at the University of Georgia. Joe Frank's father said, "That little school at Goodyear just ran through the seventh grade, and it just gave the basics. They weren't all that good, but all the mills at that time had schools."[31]

In 1866, just after the Civil War, citizens of Cartersville wanted a cotton mill or woolen manufacturing company along the banks of the Etowah River; the dream was not realized until 1903, when prominent citizen Paul Gilreath saw an ad in the *Atlanta Constitution* from E.L. McClain Manufacturing Company of Greenfield, Ohio.[32]

The worn letters on the fading Atco building deceive us into thinking it is older than it actually is. The date should read 1904, while it looks like 1804. *Bartow History Museum.*

American Textile Company (ATCO), later bought by Goodyear, made tire textiles. *Bartow History Museum.*

Tire names are street names in Atco, Georgia, such as "Mayflower" and "All Weather." *Author's collection.*

Two years later, Mr. Gilreath sought different places in the South and settled on a farm owned by Judge Akin. The farm was northwest of Cartersville between the Pettit and Nancy Creeks. They broke ground in June 1903, and the mill and the village were built on four hundred acres of prime farmland.

The E.L. McLain Manufacturing Company built a three-story red brick cotton mill with a basement for shafting and pulleys with a boiler room to run the new mill. The plan was to build seventy-five to one hundred cottages for working families. The mill would employ hundreds from the Cartersville area to make the sheeting and drills for horse collars and pads. The Greenfield, Ohio plant had been making these items on a large scale for twenty years.

By 1917, the mill boasted 350 workers. Men and women were equally represented in the mill's workforce. The mill's policy was to pay well in order to attract competent workers. Within seven months, the employees had received four raises in salary.

After a while, the horse collar business dwindled, and the mill in Cartersville retooled for the automobile industry. In 1928, Goodyear Tire and Rubber Company purchased the mill and changed the name to the American Tire

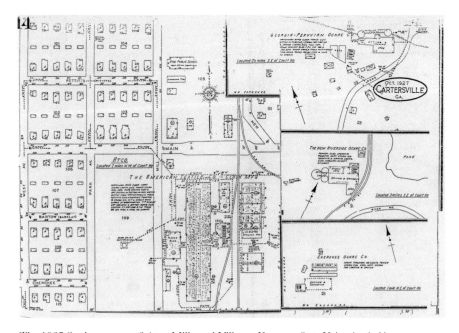

The 1927 Sanborn map of Atco Mills and Village. *Kennesaw State University Archives.*

Company, or Atco for short. Under Goodyear, the mill prospered. The village grew to almost three hundred (mostly new) houses. The company was producing tire cord for the growing automotive industry.

A Mill Village Legacy

Life in the village was unique. Sandy Moore of the Bartow History Museum interviewed Grady Jack Bryson Jr. His family moved in 1946 from the Echota Mill Village to Atco. He felt that Atco had the better mill village: "I might add that of all the places we had ever lived, the Atco Village with its amenities was the finest thing we had ever seen in our lifetime up to that time."

Bryson continued, "The first one we moved into was bigger than the houses we ordinarily lived in the mill villages. It was a four-room house. Of course, they didn't have running water in the house. We had a hydrant in the backyard. The bathroom was out back in what they called the 'cold house'—

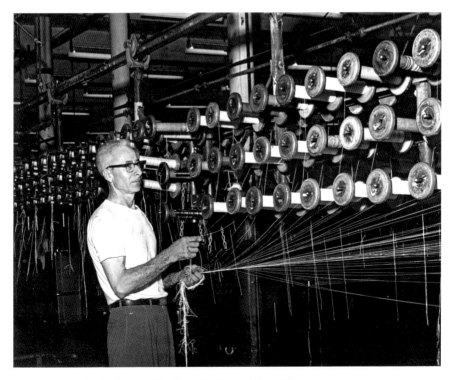

An Atco operative in Cartersville, Georgia. *Bartow History Museum.*

The remains of an Atco activity center in 2019. *Author's collection.*

you know? It was a nice bathroom with water, flushing facilities. You know, the company even furnished the toilet tissue for the bathrooms. They had a man that went around once a week and replenished the supplies."

He added, "The village itself was like a little city within itself. We had our own policeman on each shift, we had a policeman that policed the village, we had a recreational director; we could go to the mill offices and check out softball bats and softballs, everything but the gloves. We could get all the stuff. We had a program for the kids in the summertime. If we had a little injury, we would go to the nurse's station at the mill, get doctored up and go right back to what we were doing. We just had it good."[33]

The *Wingfoot Clan*

The baseball games were reported in the local newspapers and in the company news. Goodyear, from Ohio, published a locally written and edited newsletter called the *Wingfoot Clan*. The newsletter informed the workers of company events, but it mostly focused on the people in the mill.

During World War II, the Goodyear employees who were serving or the family members were featured. For example, a 1942 edition of the *Wingfoot Clan* reads, "Another promotion of interest to Goodyearites is that of former Private Lawrence Collins of Camp Bowie, Texas, who has been elevated to the Corporal of a tank unit. Lawrence is the son of Mr. Ben Collins of the Carding Department." A promotion of buying war bonds encourages workers to contribute to the war effort with a "Billion-a-Month for Victory" campaign.[34]

THE WINGFOOT CLAN

=== ATCO EDITION ===

PROTECT OUR GOOD NAME

VOL. 1   ATCO, GA., FRIDAY, JULY 25, 1930   NO. 8

SUGGESTION PLAN TO BE ADOPTED AUGUST 1st

Employees Will Be Awarded Cash For Ideas Submitted

Employees Given Opportunity To Make Extra Money. Can Show Ability to Management—Chance To Grow With Organization

SUGGESTION BOX IN LOBBY

Employees of Goodyear Clearwater Mill No. Three are again presented with a golden opportunity. One that will give every employee in this mill a chance to make some extra money, and bring him or her before the eyes of the management.

The Suggestion System

The Suggestion System, now in effect in the majority of Goodyear Mills, will be put into operation at this mill, becoming effective August 1, 1930. The Suggestion System amounts to nothing more or less than the following:

Suppose that John Doe is working in the Card Room on frames. It is understood that he is quite familiar with the job. He has a suggestion that, if his idea was put into effect, it would mean a saving to the company, and at the same time would make his job easier.

Thoughts of this kind have entered employees' minds often, but there being no suggestion department to take the suggestion up with, it didn't get any far'her than the idea. This will no longer be the case, as the Suggestion Department will review every suggestion weekly, and all suggestions submitted that can show the company a saving in dollars and cents will be awarded according to the rules and regulations of the Suggestion Department.

The Procedure

A suggestion box will be located conveniently in the Employment Office lobby. A supply of forms will be kept in this box to be used by the suggestor. After you have put your suggestion on paper, sign your name, fold and seal it, and drop in suggestion box. The suggestion will be taken up the next day by the Suggestion Department. They will, in turn, re-write on typewriter, sending one copy to the suggestor, and one to each member of the Suggestion Committee.

After the suggestion is reviewed by the committee it will be returned to the Suggestion Department with their comments. The committee will then decide if it is worth adopting and, if it is, a vote will be taken to determine what the suggestor should be rewarded for the suggestion.

All employees, who are in a supervisional capacity that submit suggestions and the suggestions fall in his regular line of duty, will not be eligible for a monetary award. However, if the idea is not in his line of duty, as determined by the chairman of the Suggestion Committee, the suggestor is then eligible for award.

Suggestion Committee

A Suggestion Committee made up of men from the mill who are well acquainted with the various operations and machinery.

Suggestion Department Will Help You

Employees who have a suggestion to offer, and have difficulty in explaining thoroughly what they have in mind are invited to call on any member of the Suggestion Committee for help.

FLOWERS BEAUTIFY THE HOME

Mrs. Dena Bott's Residence

"Neat Home Contest" Prizes Will Be Displayed

Housewives Taking Greater Interest as Contest Passes Halfway Mark—"No Room for Dirt In Atco," Says Women

Just 1st, saw the fourth month for the "Neat Home Contest." The results, which showed up very well, with a few exceptions, speaks well for our village folks. Practically every family now in Atco are real lovers of good homes, and the thought of winning one of the handsome prizes has added additional interest in the homes.

Goodyear Avenue Shows Up

Goodyear Avenue, no doubt have a harder job of keeping their premises clean than any of their neighbors due to the heavy traffic and other transit. However, with such good housekeepers, as Mrs. York, Mrs. Clark Ray, Mrs. C. G. Looney, Mrs. Duncan, and Mrs. Will Hart, the chances are that it is going to be one of our prize streets.

Despite the hot sun and bare lawns, the housewives in the new village have taken great interest in their homes. Several have planted honeysuckle vines that have circled the porches making a good shade. Many others have beautiful flowers to all of which is making Atco a healthier, happier place in which to live.

Volunteer Street

Perhaps the most noticeable change in the looks of any one street is that of Volunteer St., formerly known as Frog Town. All the houses have been freshly painted. The front and back yards are always free from trash, etc. Housewives are invited to look over this little settlement on Volunteer Street.

Garbage

During hot weather we have more or less garbage to dispose of, such as watermelons, corn husks, potato peelings, etc. All of these are very inviting to Mr. Fly. Let's all keep the flies out of our yards, as they carry many dreadful diseases. Keep lid on cans.

BEAUTIFUL GOODYEAR PARK

One of the many attractive places in the village is the beautiful park, with its many trees, abundant shrubbery and spacious lawn.

This July 1930 issue of the company newsletter, *Wingfoot Clan*, was concerned with the company image. Contests for beautifying the home and showing the Goodyear park's greenspace improvements were part of protecting the name of Goodyear. One insensitive article seems to cut against the idea of a perfect image: a picture of a young girl labeled "The biggest girl in the village." *Bartow History Museum*.

The company shares how the Goodyear rafts saved naval flyers, "Builders of Goodyear pneumatic boats must have experienced a thrill of joy and satisfaction when they saw the newspaper accounts and pictures of the rescue of three navy fliers who had been afloat in one of the 'rubber rafts' for 34 days after their plane had been forced down in the Pacific." This was an attempt to encourage workers to believe that what they do matters.

The newsletter also brought bad news. From the same first page of the *Wingfoot Clan*, "James W. Brown, brother of Mrs. Hoyt Green, became the first Bartow County Man to be lost in the service of his country in World War II."[35] The company newsletter was specialized for each mill. Goodyear in Rockmart had its own edition, but all was approved by the corporate office in Ohio.

The workers were recognized for offering suggestions to the mill and years of service. The paper asked workers to promote their products. The editors focused on village events like Twister baseball games, other sport teams and scouting. The *Wingfoot Clan* was a detailed village newspaper that ignored one event.

An article about the General Textile Strike of 1934 could not be found in the village news. Atco was part of the strike. The mill was overrun with outsiders called "Flying Squadrons" trying to cause the workers to leave the mill floor and strike. The Georgia National Guard was called and posted at the gates of Atco. At Atco, no blood was shed, and while they closed the mill temporarily, not much changed. It was certainly not mentioned in the newsletter.

The newsletters, preserved by the Bartow History Museum in Cartersville, are not always politically correct for today's sensibilities. While fishermen's daily catches were recorded and company band concerts were announced, something was missing. The absence of African Americans is not an accident. The village was for whites only. Although black laborers worked in the mill at lower grunt positions, they did not live in the village. Another article showed insensitivity.

An article a 1926 edition of the *Wingfoot Clan* announced something unusual. The newsletter was full of talent contests, cutest baby contests and beauty contest winners. I am not sure why Emma Gillespie allowed her picture to be published alongside this honor: "Emma Gillespie is Atco's largest girl. She is 14 years old, weighs 290 pounds, and is in the seventh grade at school."[36] I guess it was a slow news day.

Ideal Cotton Mill at Atco

On September 14, 1911, a writer from the *Carroll Free Press* out of Carrollton, Georgia, painted a beautiful picture in his article, titled "Georgia Weekly Press Association Party Visits Ideal Cotton Mill at Atco: Georgia Editors One and All Express Themselves as Delighted with Ideal Conditions Found in Mill, and Handsome Park-like Community. Short Story of Atco and Its Mill." The article goes way back in history: "Even while the Cherokees possessed the territory, the whites looked with longing eyes on this beautiful scope of country." Apparently, at least one of the "whites," a Scotsman named Pettit, was looking at more than the countryside. The article continues in a politically incorrect tone: "A Scotsman named Pettit, married a squaw and built himself a house near the run of the creek that now bears his name." The description continues:

When the traveler crosses the bridge over Pettit Creek on the Western and Atlantic, if he will look out of the car windows, on the left hand, if he's

The Atco Company Store is where workers bought groceries with cash, tokens or credit. Some mill residents were always in debt to the mill store. *Bartow History Museum.*

going from Atlanta to Chattanooga, he will discover a beautiful little town which has sprung into being as if by magic, and which has been laid out and built with such accuracy and elegance that he will be delighted as well as surprised to see it. This transformational scene would impress even the dullest minds.

The mill was only a few years old. If you would make the same trip today, you would not see magic—you would see historic. In 1911, this reviewer explained that the more than one hundred cottages have character, "no two being alike." Each house had privacy and separate rooms. Running water was near the kitchen door. The article did not mention the outhouses at all, but it describes how sanitary the entire town looks.

The conveniences abound within plenty of greenspace and communal cow pastures and gardens. And what you cannot grow, the company store can supply. The Atco store, "a corporation having no connection with the mill, operates a large department store in the village, affording everything of the best at moderate prices. There is also a modern barber shop with hot and cold baths in connection." The article might have been written by a modern marketer.[37]

Everything Changes

Like many manufacturers of the era, mill village homes were sold to private owners in 1958. The City of Cartersville annexed Atco on December 2, 1957. The post office was closed. Goodyear, like many mills at the time, began selling the houses. Atco was no longer a mill village, but the sense of community remained.

On October 1, 2003, Goodyear closed the mill doors in Atco, leaving the remaining 319 employees out of work. According to the *Rome News-Tribune* writer, an effort was made to list the mills and homes on the National Register of Historic Places beginning in 2002. Atco won the designation on October 21, 2005.

The plant is slowly disappearing. What remains is a shadow of a productive industry—a precarious water tower and the last pieces of a mill that bears its birthdate of 1904. With everything else torn down around that section of the old mill, that one section is resistant to the wrecking ball. It is reluctant to go.[38]

What remains of Atco in 2019. *Author's collection.*

Atco Water Tower, a lonely remnant on the mill property. *Author's collection.*

Chapter 3

Chattooga County

BERRYTON

Raccoon Creek Mills, 1883

"He sips." Georgia's ninety-third county was named from the river bubbling up near LaFayette in Walker County and rolling southwest into Alabama. The real translation of Chattooga has been lost. Some say it is a Cherokee phrase, *tsatu-gi*, with these possible meanings: "has crossed the river," "drank by sips" or "he sips." Others say that it is not Cherokee at all, which is ironic if the rumor is true that Sequoia, the inventor of the Cherokee alphabet, was born in Chattooga.

The large Cherokee village on the Chattooga was known as Chattooga, one of six large settlements with names recognizable today and some lost to history: Island Town, Dirt Town, White Oak Town, Broom Town and Raccoon Town. Before 1830, Chattooga and the other settlements were part of the very large county called Cherokee. Cherokee was divided into ten smaller counties. Realizing that the area was too large to manage, another county was formed in 1838: Chattooga. On January 28, 1839, the citizens of the new county elected its first officers, but the two-story brick courthouse was not built until 1909.[39]

Raccoon Town grew up on the banks of Raccoon Creek. A tiny Cherokee village, Raccoon Town began where Raccoon Creek empties into the Chattooga River. The original dwellings must have been scattered, but the greatest concentration was where the Summerville filter plant is now located. At first there was a gristmill on Raccoon Creek, and then a post office opened in 1877, with Joseph M. Wyatt as the first postmaster.

In 1883, Raccoon Cotton Mills (later known as Raccoon Manufacturing Company) opened when the population of the town was only 441. Many residents worked at the mills, operating 104 looms and 3,400 spindles. The Raccoon Cotton Mills went bankrupt just before the turn of the century, and John M. Berry rescued the mills and the town.[40]

John Berry owned Rome Hosiery Mills. The *West Georgia Textile Trail* reported that in 1910, Berry purchased Raccoon Manufacturing Company and named the mills and the town Berryton after himself. Berry "used the mill's 5,000 spindles and 200 workers to produce yarn for Rome Hosiery Mills and other mills in the area. Berry made extensive improvements and alterations to the mill, which operated by steam and waterpower and contained 5,000 ring spindles and 100 knitting machines."[41]

The company also owned the mill village. It charged twenty-five cents per room for the one hundred mill village houses, and sometimes two families shared one home. Attempting to take care of its people, Berryton mill village contained a mill-owned company store where residents could barter for goods. The community connected with the rest of North Georgia by a railroad line coming close to the village. The mill *was* Berryton. Labor disputes outside did not impact the town—that is, not until 1951.

While another Chattooga county mill and neighboring Floyd County mills were enmeshed in the 1934 textile millworkers' uprising, Berryton was not affected. However, in 1951, during the Textile Workers of America Strike, one nonstriking female employee was killed.

Owner John M. Berry died in 1952, and the mill conditions worsened. A North Carolina company, Harriet & Henderson, purchased the mill from the Berry family in 1958 and operated it until 2000, when the mill closed.[42]

SUMMERVILLE

Summerville Cotton Mills, 1907

If you visit Summerville, you will see the textile industry thriving in the twenty-first century. The methods have changed, but one hundred years later, Summerville is still producing textiles. Mills have changed hands and the village is a thing of the past, but Mohawk Industries still employs Chattooga residents to produce carpet.

In Summerville, Mohawk's modern mill converts discarded water bottles into plastic pellets that become carpet fiber. Mohawk reclaims more than 3 billion plastic bottles each year and recycles them into PET chips that eventually become carpet fiber. A community of workers sorts through plastic bottles of all shapes, sizes and colors and then grinds them into useable pellets.[43] Times have changed, but the mill lifestyle continues in Summerville.

The railroad arrived in the county seat in 1899, and Summerville flipped from an agricultural area to textile town. The first mill, Summerville Cotton Mill, opened in 1907. Workers put out coarse and durable cotton products such as duck, osnaburg and awning cloth. The company did well. Electricity came to the mill in 1916, initiating the night shifts. The Summerville Cotton Mill expanded tripling production.

The growth of Summerville is credited to the Summerville Cotton Mills. As reported in 1917 in an *Atlanta Constitution* article, "Back in 1907, before the Summerville Cotton Mills were in existence, Summerville in Chattooga County, Georgia, was merely a dot in comparison with what it is now."[44] The Atlanta paper attributed its growth and success to the company policy of "co-operation." The town felt like it owned the mill—it was "our mill," not "their mill." Exactly what management wanted.

By 1917, the Summerville Mills village contained seventy homes on large lots. The homes were "new and neatly painted," according to the *Atlanta Constitution*. The mention of trees "to be found everywhere" and flowers not only in the yard but on porches reminds us that North Georgia was once barren of trees in some locations brought on by erosion and construction. The sidewalks were paved, and the mill maintained a private water system. The mill set aside a seventy-five-acre plot for garden spots and a place for the family pig or cow. According to the *West Georgia Textile Trail*, "The mill owners provided an African American groundskeeper and a mule to keep the grounds maintained for the mill operatives."[45]

Mr. John D. Taylor, president and treasurer of Summerville Cotton Mills, said that the mill village had twenty private homes—bought by the operatives in the last ten years of operation. Taylor encouraged his people to buy their own homes. He noted, "Just like anywhere else, if a person owns his home, he naturally feels more interest in the place and will do more to make it the best possible." Taylor gathered the male operatives together and told them that if they wanted to buy their own homes, he would furnish the money. His motto: "We are all partners in the business."[46]

The mill did not have a doctor or nurse in the 1917 mill town, but if someone was "taken ill," a nurse was employed to stay as long as necessary at the mill's expense. The attitude was that the mill children should have all the advantages of town children with excellent schools. While there was a church in the village, the mill officials asked them to attend the churches in Summerville, "for the people at Summerville are very lovely to the mill people and would like to have them in the churches."[47] According to the *Atlanta Constitution* in 1917, just ten years after Summerville Cotton Mills opened:

> *Some people have the idea that a cotton mill is the most awful place in the world to gain one's livelihood, that there is no fresh air, that the operatives are always crowded and no freedom is found, but I just wish you would pay a visit to this mill. You would certainly have to change your mind no matter how prejudiced you may have been beforehand, for there is plenty of light and fresh air and space for free movements; the machines are from being crowded together.*[48]

This early *Atlanta Constitution* article may have been part propaganda, but it gives a glimpse of what was happening in at least one North Georgia mill town. The mill owners wanted to be known as the worker's partner, but they acted like a paternalistic "Papa."[49]

In 1935, the effects of the Depression caused this once prosperous mill to go bankrupt. The mill changed hands often. The business was auctioned in 1938. During World War II, the mill was resurrected to deliver military uniforms and stayed alive for years. However, in 1980, following the textile pattern of North Georgia, Summerville Mills closed the doors and demolished most of the buildings.

Many other Summerville textile mills survived with different products and purposes, but the Summerville Cotton Mills was gone. While mill homes remain, the purpose of the community is lost to history.[50]

TRION/RIEGEL/MOUNT VERNON

Trion Factory/Trion, 1847

The oldest and longest-running mill in Northwest Georgia has quite a past. The tales of Trion in Chattooga County include murder, mayhem, fighting, flames, strikes, soldiers and finally rebuilding and repurposing. The town was codependent on the mill, and its inception is woven into the fabric of the history of a place called Trion Factory.

Andrew Allgood came to Chattooga County and set up a business. Spencer Marsh began a similar business about the same time. Instead of becoming enemies, they worked together. They gathered as much capital as they could and found in William K. Briers of LaFayette a third party to be a silent, contributing partner. Eventually, Allgood bought Briers out, but in the beginning, this trio planted a cotton mill in the middle of Island Town. Island Town became Trion Factory in honor of the three entrepreneurs. The unincorporated town stretched one mile in all directions from the mill, but not until the Georgia legislature passed an act on December 9, 1862, was Trion Factory incorporated.[51]

Only two other North Georgia cotton mills were up and running at the time: Manchester Mills in Douglas County and Roswell Mills in Cobb County. Both were destroyed by the invading Union armies. Roswell opened in 1839 and produced the famous "Roswell Gray" worn by Rebel troops. These mills shared the early textile history with Trion, but each had a different war experience.

The Secret Southern Yankee

The reason for the reprieve was left a mystery until documents surfaced. Stories conflict about why the Trion Cotton Mills were spared William Tecumseh Sherman's torch. The best information is from the people who were there. In a letter found among the Cooper family papers is an account written by Alice Allgood Cooper on Trion Factory letterhead, Cooper's mother, Mary Ann Marsh Allgood, remembered the night in 1864 when Sherman and his staff arrived at the Allgood home in Trion, Georgia[52]:

> *Sherman and staff arrived and spent the night. Among the staff were Generals O.O. Howard and Oslinhaus. For supper I gave him bacon, biscuits, cornbread and coffee—which was all I had and said to General Sherman, "I am giving you all that your men have left me." He said that he would furnish me with food, but of course I declined to accept any of his aid; then as he and Howard were talking of the proposed march through Georgia he said, "We will be easy on this part of the state, but when we*

get to Middle Georgia—we will hike the bridles off and if a crow wants to come in, it will have to bring its rations under its wings."

The men took any and everything that could be carried away, even the silk stockings which I had packed away.[53]

Mrs. Allgood also remembered when the Confederates visited her home:

General Wheeler, who was retreating with his staff before the advance of Sherman's army, spent the night here; they had thrown away everything, and were literally in "light marching order" and asked me if I could have their shirts washed and dried during the night. Of course, I gladly consented; but as the flannel shirts were not quite dry by breakfast, they came down with their coats buttoned up, but before they could sit down to the table, Sherman's advance guard began firing on their outpost. General Wheeler and staff took as much of the breakfast as they could, rolled up their damp shirts; and fled.

A little later a Federal Captain rode up, called me out, and asked how many men Wheeler had; upon my telling him that I did not know, he replied, "I did not expect the truth when I asked you.[54]

Mary Ann's story was confirmed by her husband, Andrew P. Allgood. Roswell Mill in Cobb County and Manchester Mills in Douglas County were completely burned, while Trion was not. In a lawsuit concerning the Manchester Mills, Allgood was required to explain why. This completes the story his wife told their daughter in transcription.

Andrew P. Allgood made the following statement on June 11, 1869: "When General Sherman passed our place in October 1864, he stayed all night with me and the next morning gave me protection papers." Allgood convinced Sherman that his factory had produced rough woolen textiles for the Confederacy under threat and that he was, in fact, a Union man. His testimony continued:

General O.O. Howard sent a large guard to the factory to protect all the property there and showed no disposition on to destroy any of our property except provisions. I took extra pains to let the Union men of the county know my status or position and rendered them all the aid I could when they were in trouble and was known as a Union Man. *We stopped running on May 10th, 1864....I worked for the Confederate government under protest.*[55]

Top: Smokestack at Trion Mills, 1895. *From wikiwand. com/en/Trion_Georgia.*

Bottom: An early aerial view of Trion Cotton Mills. *Trion Public Library.*

Before the war, Allgood quietly disapproved of secession, but he did not come out unscathed by declaring his allegiance to the Union. The townspeople tried to hang him, but his beard was too thick; he escaped the noose. Just over ten years later, on April 10, 1876, Trion Factory burned. Arson was suspected—maybe by Confederate loyalists in the town—but it only shut the doors for six months.

Later, Allgood became a reluctant elected judge. In an 1898 article, the author Miss Edna Cain noted that Judge A.P. Allgood was a "distinctive businessman and a pioneer." She used the Trion Mills as an example of a successful cotton mill.[56]

The mill was running successfully by 1880, but Judge A.P. Allgood was in poor health. He raised his only son, Deforrest, from a young age to be a "thorough mill man." The twenty-four-year-old was in charge of one of the largest cotton mills in Georgia. Under the younger Allgood, the mill prospered and doubled production from his father's years as president. He lived in Trion but visited Rome often. He was known to be "generous, noble-hearted with engaging manners" In Trion, Deforrest (or "Deedy," as he was known) was loved because he took care of the families in his mill village. He whitewashed their houses every spring and gave each family a garden and showed them how to work it.[57]

Ten years had passed since Deforrest took over the Trion Mill for his father. He married, built a home near his father's and found a wife. His four sisters also were living in Trion. One of his sisters, Addie, married a doctor and moved to Rome.

A Frightful Tragedy in Rome

The headline shouts from the *Atlanta Constitution* on January 21, 1890: "Allgood Shot Dead: By Dr. J.B.S. Holmes, His Brother-in-Law." On a winter night in Rome, Georgia, Deforrest Allgood, president of Trion Factory, was shot and killed by a prominent physician, his brother-in-law.

The Atlanta paper reported that Allgood came down from Trion Factory to Rome on the evening train and waited for Holmes in his office door. The paper continued, "Holmes had avoided Allgood for years, and went out of town to avoid meeting him today." Holmes, as the paper noted, "had a vague warning, sought to reach his office by back streets." He had been out hunting with friends.[58]

When the party arrived at Holmes's office, Allgood was waiting with pistol drawn. In self-defense, Holmes shot Allgood with a double-barreled shotgun loaded with birdshot. The paper was graphic: "Both shots taking effect, the first cutting the carotid artery and the jugular vein, and the second breaking the neck completely." Allgood fell on the first shot and then rose slightly, "still trying to draw his pistol. When he received the second shot he fell on his face, and instantly expired."[59]

Holmes surrendered to the deputy sheriff. According to the *Atlanta Constitution* one day after the shooting, Holmes claimed self-defense: "I was forced to do it to save my own life. I am sorry, so sorry, but he hunted me down, and for the sake of my wife and my son I had to kill him."[60]

Both men were popular figures, and after the shooting, Rome supported Dr. Holmes. He came to Rome in 1870 to work with his uncle, Dr. G.W. Holmes. He later opened his own practice and married Addie Allgood. He built a large and successful practice in Rome.[61]

CHATTOOGANS IDENTIFIED IN 105-YEAR-OLD PICTURE

In the Centennial Edition of the Trion Facts on Oct. 11, 1945, an old picture appeared in which the principals shown were un-identified. Now, Ross Bruce of Route 1, Trion, has made an identi-fication of the three men in the picture, which was taken about 1865. The man on the left is Jake Worthy (his wife was Caroline Hanes Worthy), grandfather of Mr. Bruce. Mr. Worthy, who was born in 1832, hauled cotton for the Trion mill from the warehouse to the opening room. He also hauled cotton from Rome to Trion. In the center is a Mr. King, who worked for Mr. Worthy. At right is DeForrest Allgood, son of Andrew P. Allgood, one of the found-ers of the Trion Co. DeForrest Allgood served as president of the company after his father's death in 1882. Much progress was made in Trion during the Eighties: the mill was enlarged, electricity was installed, and the railroad was completed through Trion. De-Forrest Allgood died in 1890. The pair of oxen shown above were named "Blue" and "Gray."

Jackson "Jake" Worthy, Mr. King and DeForrest Allgood (son of A.P. Allgood). Allgood was the president after A.P. died. DeForrest was shot by his brother-in-law.

An eyewitness to the shooting was a friend of both men. He tried to calm Allgood the night of the incident and asked him to settle his differences with Holmes peacefully. Allgood was said to be a high-strung individual and was certain that Holmes was trying to oust him from his position at Trion Mill. The paper recorded the eyewitness who was trying to talk Allgood down, saying that Allgood was angry: "No, by God, I'll settle it my own way. This shall settle it," drawing his revolver and flourishing it. When Holmes's carriage was heard driving up, Allgood remarked, "There comes the damned scoundrel, now."[62]

Holmes was acquitted of murder charges. Rome residents were certain that Dr. Holmes was innocent. The people in Trion believed that President Allgood did nothing to provoke Holmes. Editorials in the Summerville paper spoke against the "not guilty" verdict.

According to the Mount Vernon Mills historical archive, "People that witnessed it attest that Mr. Allgood's favorite horses refused to pull the hearse that was to bear his body and that in the midst of the funeral new horses had to be brought in."[63] Another brother-in-law became the president of Trion Manufacturing Company.

A New Family in Town

In 1893, Mr. Alfred Shorter Hamilton (married to Margaret Allgood) installed a large bell—known as the Deforrest Allgood Memorial Bell—and placed it in the tower of a new mill. The new 1,028-pound bell was used to wake the workers each weekday morning and on Sunday.[64] Hamilton brought automatic sprinklers for the warehouse, new homes and a new Baptist church.

Child labor was an issue at Trion, despite what Hamilton said. Miss Edna Caine spoke highly of Hamilton's treatment of children in his mill:

> President Hamilton of Trion company, who has given these matters much thought, assures me that he prefers not to employ child labor. But there are people entirely unable to support their large sole purpose of increasing their income with the wages of their children. Widows who cannot support their children come here with them. And it would seem a mistake to legislate against it, for if this disease of poverty is checked here it will break out elsewhere.[65]

In 1895, an ice factory opened, and a soda fountain was installed. And just five years later, Hamilton built Mill No. 3. That was not to last. Alfred Shorter Hamilton was accused of embezzling funds, and the fourth-largest mill in the state in 1901 was in decline and forced into bankruptcy by 1912.

The mill was put into receivership, and well-known Roman John Paul Cooper was placed in temporary control of the Trion Manufacturing Company. Cooper, another brother-in-law, was married to another Allgood daughter, Alice. The newly formed company, the Trion Company, was purchased by another family, the Riegels. Benjamin D. Riegel, a New York businessman, brought the company into the new century with many improvements to the town and the mill village. He had muddy streets paved and refurbished the mill housing. He turned the old company store into a modern department store that became known as the "Bos Dissatisfaction."

More Tragedy in Trion, 1934

The oldest and longest continuously running mill only shut down for a few reasons. The mill was used as a hospital in 1858. After Allgood's encounter with Sherman, he agreed to close the doors until the end of the war in exchange for 1864 letters of protection. And in 1934, when the General Textile Strike hit Trion, the mill shuttered for six weeks.[66]

Outsiders came to Trion in late August 1934 in preparation for the General Textile Strike, set to begin on Labor Day. The "Flying Squadron" was made up of striking textile workers coming to rural Georgia mills who were not unionized. Their mission was to stir up union support and encourage workers to walk out and close it down. On September 9, 1934, Trion had its first strike. The Stove and Iron workers of Rome, along with the "Flying Squadrons" from other towns, forced a strike, described by mill official "Sadd" Dalton as "being just like a war."[67]

The Trion Company had good relationships between management and worker. The family owners all tried to improve the lives of the workers. Andrew Allgood built the mill village and kept the mill going through difficult times. He rebuilt after a fire and only closed the mill for a short time. His son, Deforrest, provided clean homes (minus the snuff and tobacco stains). He provided garden beds and whitewashed all the homes. He was instrumental in bringing the railroad to Trion on July 4, 1888. He was beloved.

Entrance to Trion Park and Glove Mill. *Author's collection.*

Reigel Mill has stayed as a family business since before the Civil War, but it has gone by various names: Trion Mill, Trion Factor and Mount Vernon Mills. *Chattooga County Historical Society.*

A.S. Hamilton installed a bell to ring in the morning to wake the employees. He added new homes and barns, a waste house, a school building, sprinklers in the warehouses and an icehouse. The *Trion Echo* said of the ice factory, "One of the most magnanimous deeds of the Trion Company is the erection of a splendid ice plant, the products which, during the summer months, add untold comfort to the people of the place....They make 1000 pounds of ice per day, the very low price of which places it within reach of all."[68]

Riegel purchased the mill and shipped home improvement materials to Trion even before he arrived from New York. He built a dairy and the Big Friendly. He provided a new eating establishment, the Riegel Tavern Inn, known beyond Trion. Riegel expanded the warehouse and built the largest work glove plant in the country. He modernized dyeing and finishing processes. He built a hospital that was available to workers for a fraction of the cost. He even got rid of the red muddy roads and lots and cemented them over. The man loved Trion. However, things changed when the 1930s Great Depression brought the New Deal. National Recovery Act (NRA) policies enforced strike wage and hour rules on manufacturers, and the management passed it along.

Workers were given fewer hours and more work. This practice was called the stretch-out. Slower workers were fired, and faster workers were given more to do. The relationship was breaking down. The workers' legitimate concerns were ignored. A group interfered in the relationship between manager and worker.

When things were heating up in September 1934, the mill owners asked the governor for help. He recommended the sheriff deputize as many as he needed. The deputies showed up at the mill with their weapons. A group came from Rome and tried to take away the deputies' guns. After taking a pistol from one deputy, Granville Ball refused to surrender his weapon to the striker. The deputy opened fired, wounding two strikers.

Vice-President N.B. Murphy asked deputies to turn in their weapons. Strikers demanded Sheriff Arthur Bloodworth arrest Deputy Ball. He tried to put them off by saying the deputy was in the mill somewhere. The mob pushed their way in to find Ball. The sheriff asked Deputy Milton Hix and Jim Young to go into the mill with him to evict the strikers.

Caption on back of photo reads: "Pickets carrying sticks, iron bars, and clubs in front of Trion Cotton Mill, Trion, Georgia." Two people were killed on this day, September 5, 1934. *Edward Levinson Collection, Wayne State University.*

National Guard troops camping in tent villages during the strike at Trion Mills. *Chattooga County Historical Society.*

The strikers outnumbered the three lawmen and rushed them. A hail of gunfire ensued, and only two strikers came out unharmed. Deputy Hix was shot during the confusion by a young boy hiding in the hallway.[69] The union members refused to allow an ambulance into the mill to get Hix. Men put him on a stretcher and carried him through the mill, across the footbridge and to the hospital. He died later that day.[70]

After the violence, Georgia Guardsmen came and set up camp at the mill. Huge bales of cotton were positioned around the mill with machine gun nests behind them. The mill managers were positioned by the soldiers to identify workers to keep others away. Workers coming to the mill were not impressed with the union, and they never unionized.[71]

The War Years

In 1941, Mr. Riegel died, and his cousin John L. Riegel led the company through the war years. The Army-Navy E Award was presented to Trion Company in 1943. At these events throughout the country, employees were asked to speak in acceptance of the award. Mr. J.M. Wooten and two others were selected. This is what he said:

It is with great pride, yet humbly, that we, the employees of Trion, accept this award which represents a hard job well done on our part as well as the part of the management. We will wear our pins proudly and we will work harder than ever to prove that these symbols of our efficiency have been honestly earned....We are glad that we have done the job as well as they say we have but I do not need to say that any time Uncle Sam needs us, the people of Trion will not falter but will cooperate to the fullest extent in order that liberty and freedom in this country will march on forever.[72]

Hauling materials from the cloth room at Trion Mills. *Chattooga County Historical Society.*

During World War II, Trion Company produced enough fabric to make 10.5 million fatigues, 11 million yards of tent twill, 10 million gun patches and 180 million gloves. The war ended and the mill continued to grow, but times were changing. More than five thousand people were employed in Trion by 1950, and many still lived in the villages.

A former resident of the Trion mill village remembered how the company took care of the homes by repairing and maintaining everything, including septic issues. Don remembered the "Dookey Wagons." He said they would come around twice a week, fill them up and deposit the waste right into the Chattooga River. Although this practice has long since ceased due to indoor plumbing, he still warns anyone from eating fish from the river. Once, something else was found in that river.

In 1896, as the eels migrated up the Chattooga River, they were stopped by the Trion dam. They turned around to go downstream and were caught in the raceway and the water wheel. The power shut down when the eels jammed the water wheel. Imagine the cleanup. Workers loaded three two-horse wagons full of dead eels for disposal.[73]

The Trion Company, following the industrial trend, sold all the homes to renters or private buyers. By 1950, the mill was no longer responsible for the mill village.[74] Instead, Trion Mills focused on expanding and upgrading in the 1950s and 1960s.

By the 1970s, according to the official history of Trion Mills, now Mount Vernon Mills, the mill that had been producing greige fabrics for 130 years was producing a yarn-dyed fabric: denim. Denim became the product that saved many mills, including Trion.[75]

A Third Family in Trion

The mills at Trion have been held by only three families since 1847: the Allgood family (1845–1912), the B.D. Riegel family (1912–87) and the R.B. Pamplin family (1987–to present).

While other mills were closing in the 1970s and 1980s, Riegel's business was steady. Trion was sold in 1985 to R.B. Pamplin Sr., one of the three original founders of Georgia Pacific, who purchased Riegel Textile Corporation. He had served on the board of directors of Mount Vernon and bought the mills after he retired. Riegel's daughter, Mrs. German H.H. Emory, was a major stockholder at the time, and she offered to sell her stock to Pamplin. She believed that he would treat the mills, the employees and the communities the way her father had. She felt that the company was in good hands.[76]

Trion Today

On a sunny afternoon driving past the mill between three and four o'clock, there is a mass exodus. The Hamilton bell might not ring anymore, but the cars are filing out after a long shift. The mill homes look on across the street, watching a redundant pattern of quitting time. The homes sit in stages of disrepair and rejuvenation.

Don Hayes grew up in the mill village but avoids returning to the area. The condition of the village is too depressing for the former Trion mayor. He can point out his old house and remember sitting on the porch looking at the mill across the street. He remembers roller skating in the park that was next to the mill. He talks about the Big Friendly, a type of mall that had everything. He said, "Everything in Trion was self-contained. There was no need to go anywhere else. We had a gym, movie theater, swimming pool and the Big Friendly."[77]

Trion mill survived the Civil War, both world wars, fires, the Depression, a major strike and three family-owners. While the mill is thriving, the mill village has not fared as well. The little town of Trion is a testimony to stamina and perseverance. Perhaps that will translate into a complete restoration of the mill village homes.

One thing is certain. The workers and the managers believed in hard work—something we have lost today. Here is a bit of advice left in the 1928 company newsletter, the *Trion Facts*:

My son, remember, you have to work. Whether you handle a pick and shovel, a set of books, or a wheelbarrow; whether, you dig ditches, edit a newspaper, ring door bells, or sell behind a counter, you must work.

Don't be afraid of killing yourself by overworking on the sunny side of thirty. Men die young sometimes, but it is generally because they stop work at 6 p.m. and don't go home until 2 a.m. It's the intervals that kill, my son. The work gives you appetite for your meals, lends solidity to your slumber, gives you perfect appreciation of a holiday.

There are young men who do not work, but the country is not proud of them. It does not even know their names; it only speaks of them as So-and-So's boys. The great busy world doesn't know they've arrived so, my son, find out what you want to be and do. Take off your coat and make dust in the world.[78]

Great advice from a father to a son in 1928, and even better advice today. The legacy of hard work was important in the Trion Mills.

CHAPTER 4

CHEROKEE COUNTY

CANTON

Canton Cotton Mills, 1901

Hidden in Canton, Georgia, are two resurrected mills, repurposed with two separate plans. Canton Cotton Mills' original purpose is lost to history, but the legacy echoes in the hills of Cherokee. You cannot talk about Canton or the Canton Mills without addressing Mr. R.T. Jones. You can almost hear his voice echo in the past: "Make it better, make it better, make it better."

The mills, the man and the town of Canton are inseparable. E.A. McCanless, a close friend and associate of R.T. Jones, said of the man, "It doesn't matter where you start this story....We just got to come back to R.T. Jones after a while." So, let's start with him.[79]

Robert Tyre Jones (1849–1937) would not like the credit local historians have given him. He said, "No man ever accomplished anything really worthwhile alone. There are always two additional forces at work—other people and Providence."

To tell the Canton story, Jones must be the protagonist. He came to Cherokee County in the late nineteenth century with the intention of only staying three years. He opened Jones Mercantile, the largest in the region. In 1899, after building a successful business, Jones helped create Canton Cotton Mills. With the railroad in town and the loss of the mining industry, the town

Canton Mills No. 1 on Railroad Street. Robert Tyre Jones, one of the major donors to start the construction, founded the Canton Cotton Mills in 1899. Golfer Bobby Jones was his grandson. *Author's collection.*

needed a strong business to grow, and the town fathers wanted a cotton mill. Jones invested $25,000 of the $75,000 needed to start construction and bring the cotton industry to Canton. On the banks of the Etowah River in 1901, a Cotton Mill using locally grown cotton was born and cotton thread was made.

Like most new business, Canton Mills had to adjust and retool, especially due to financial setbacks in 1902; it constructed a dye house to begin making denim. This became its signature product until the mill closed in the 1980s. Jones was a leader in the industry. A speech he gave to a group of textile mill owners was published in the *Cherokee Advance.* On December 25, 1903, Jones shared his opinions on the price of cotton and shutdowns, "I am opposed to curtailing production from every stand point." He continued: "The only solution to the situation in my judgement is to raise the price of goods so that we can work high cotton at a profit."[80]

Jones's speech sounded a little like price fixing. At that time, antitrust laws were not enforced, and it was still legal to manage the market as Jones suggested. He overcame the difficulties of 1902 and switched from producing cotton sheeting to the new and profitable denim market. Jones and his mill became important in the textile industry. He filled government contracts for World War I and continued to make the mill profitable. The company expanded by building a second plant in Canton.

Mill No. 2 was built in 1923 along with another mill village to support the growth. The 750 looms and 23,000 spindles of Mill No. 2 produced fine denim famous for its quality and durability. The primary buyer at this time was the Levi-Strauss Company.

Always innovating and improving, Canton Mills was among the first textile plants to install a sanforizing machine in 1935. Sanforized denim is made by putting the cloth through a stretching and shrinking process to reduce shrinkage on jeans of only 1–3 percent as opposed to 10 percent shrinkage with un-sanforized (shrink to fit) denim. Within a few years and many sanforizing machines later, 85 percent of the materials produced were sanforized.

During World War II, the mill delivered low-grade cotton tent twill for the war effort. After the war, the growth continued. Even though R.T. Jones died in 1937, workers continued to hear his voice: "Make it better, make it better, make it better."

Mill No. 2 received an addition in the 1950s, doubling its capacity to produce denim. Modernization and reorganization began in the early 1960s. New automated equipment added synthetic fibers, changing the name from Canton Cotton Mills to Canton Textile Mills. In the 1970s, polyester was becoming dominant over cotton.[81]

For the first fifty years of operation, Canton Cotton Mills never shut down. During the Great Depression, when businesses shuttered their doors, Canton Cotton Mills employed frugality in business and developed a tough resistance to hard economic times. It used local resources—local cotton farmers—and made it work.

Canton Mills No. 2, 1940. This second mill was built in 1923 as a three-story building. There was an attached one-story brick dye house and several brick warehouses. The mills closed in 1981 and have since been repurposed as loft apartments. *Cherokee Historical Society.*

Mill village under construction in Canton, Georgia. *Cherokee Historical Society.*

Even in 1934, when mills were forced to close due to the nationwide textile workers strike, Canton Cotton Mill did not shut down. The workers did not want to strike because they were treated well by the owners.[82]

The town grew with new jobs, and by 1939, Canton had grown in population—2,893 due in great part to the mills at Canton. The growth was supported because workers had a home. Jones built a village. Copying from the mining industry that had come and gone in Cherokee County, Jones constructed homes, schools and churches for his operatives. Jones Mercantile, now run by his son, was in practicality the company store. Mr. Jones even conceived of a mass transportation system for the daily commutes of his workers.[83]

Both mills built homes for their employees, and the mill village featured amenities such as indoor plumbing, running water, electricity and ice delivery. Jones Mercantile Store, owned and operated by one of R.T. Jones's sons, became a popular shop for the residents of the Canton Cotton Mills villages.

No evidence exists about why Jones originally came to Canton. He had only intended to stay three years, but he was very clear why he stayed. He fell in love with the wildness of the Appalachian foothills in Cherokee County. Jones added so much to this region and helped it to grow. He never wanted to go anywhere else. As he aged, his doctor suggested a long vacation. Jones said, "Why? Where else would I be as happy?? I came to Canton to stay for three years. The longer I stayed the better I like it. I just want to go on staying here. I do not want to go to Atlantic City, or New York, or Florida or Heaven—or anywhere else."[84]

Canton Cotton Mills had difficulties beginning in 1902, as well as during the Great Depression: the threat of striking workers, floods and changes in leadership. However, it was the cheaper international markets in the late 1970s that finally closed Canton Cotton Mills in 1981.

The Canton Mills were important to North Georgia industry. The mill provided jobs for almost one-third of the area. Many Cherokee County residents were unemployed, but the same year the mill closed, Interstate 575 opened Canton to metro Atlanta, creating an easy commute. The mill closed, but not forever.

Rebuilding and Repurposing Two Mills

In 1981, the mill closed. Canton Cotton Mill No. 2 is significant in the area of architecture as a good example of an early twentieth-century textile mill. The main mill building and dye house retain their brick and heavy-timber construction, fenestration and industrial features. The warehouses retain their brick and wood construction and concrete floors. The building is described in an application for inclusion in the National Register of Historic Places:

> The main mill building is of heavy-timber construction with load-bearing brick walls. Three towers are attached on the south façade and two on the west façade. The fenestration consists of one rectangular window in each bay on each floor. The interior of the building features an open plan with wood columns and beams and maple floors.[85]

One hundred years after Canton Mills opened (1899), Mill No. 2 was repurposed into loft-style apartments. The brick walls of the mill are exposed, and the ductwork is unhidden in the studio and one- and two-bedroom apartments. Reopened in 1999, the Canton Mill Lofts have changed management and added even more restoration, providing amenities for the twentysomething consumer. Some reports say the old textile mill is haunted. If those walls could speak….

In an *Atlanta Journal* special report, H.M. Cauley wrote about when Mill No. 2 opened for business. "A second mill opened in 1924, and from then through the 1960s, workers flocked to Canton from nearby cities to put in long shifts in hot, high-ceilinged rooms where the air was flocked with lint specks. In later years, their labor turned raw cotton into scrubbed denim." Now young adults live in those places where people worked so hard to make a living. They lived in the bungalows across from the mill and were given an opportunity to purchase those small homes in the 1960s for $4,000.[86]

What about the first mill on Railroad Street in Canton, the original 1899 building? This location housed a few businesses, but nothing to draw people. It remained hidden until 2019, when the land was purchased for redevelopment. Visions of a multipurpose facility along the Etowah River are becoming a reality.

Robert Tyre Jones founded and financed the Canton Cotton Mills in 1899, and the mill opened in 1900. After more than eighty years of producing textiles for the military and mainly denims, his descendants repurposed the building to serve as warehouse and production space for local tenants for thirty years. In 2018, a group of local developers bought the property to revitalize the area and remain true to the legacy. The Mill on Etowah was reborn. One of the businesses is moving production to the site.[87]

Reformation Brewery is relocating to the Mill on Etowah, and the owner is slightly poetic about the move to Canton. Owner Spencer Nicks commented, "We exist to be part of people's stories….Canton has a beautiful story…and in some ways it is just being reborn…and just to be a chapter in that story is awesome."[88]

Canton Mills No. 1 under restoration. An area developer purchased this mill property to resurrect it for shops, restaurants, offices and residences. *Author's collection.*

Canton Mills No. 1 being repurposed and rebranded as Canton Mills, with greenspace and river access. The property will be used for bike trails and walking, calling it the "Canton Loop." *Author's collection.*

Canton Mills village house in 2019. It is unclear if these homes will survive remodeling of the Canton Mills project. *Author's collection.*

The Jones family have supported the legacy of the Canton Mills through the Cherokee County Historical Society and encouraged of the reuse of the mills. The Canton Mill Lofts house many young adults starting out, and the new Mill on Etowah will give many small businesses new homes. The admonition for these new enterprises of lofts and shops comes from the original builder. Mr. R.T. Jones's voice whispers to the present developers; he would never settle for second best. He reminds them, "Make it better, make it better, make it better."

Chapter 5

Cobb County

CLARKDALE

Coats and Clark Thread Mills, 1904

The Clarkdale community has the designation of the last mill village developed in Georgia. This factory town was built in the early 1930s, when Coats and Clark moved manufacturing South. The historical marker reports that Clarkdale is significant as an intact industrial village, locally called a mill village. Built according to a master plan for the employees of the Clark Thread Company, this self-contained community had a bowling alley, a theater, a baseball team and low-rent housing provided by the mill. The homes were modern with electricity and indoor plumbing, and in 1945 automobile garages were added. The village had 138 units, and it cost eight dollars per month for a four-room house. The company owned and cared for the homes, but the businesses were privately owned.[89]

Piece of Scotland in the South

The Clark Thread Company began two hundred years ago. Cotton thread began in the town of Paisley, Scotland. Another Paisley man, James Coats, brought his yarn twisting to the thread business. Coats died, and his sons,

James and Peter, took over and formed J&P Coats. In 1896, Coats and Clark joined interests, but they kept their separate identities. In 1931, the two companies completely joined and moved south.

The Scottish textile company bought the old Acworth Hosiery Mill in 1904. It built the community of Clarkdale in Austell, Georgia, as the last planned community in 1932. The Coats and Clark thread mill was built on top of the hill with 138 homes circling on winding, tree-lined roads.

The company built recreation into the plan, but the employees added more. In 1950, a civic group in the mill dug Pine View Lake and stocked it with fish.[90]

Once layoffs at the mill started in the late 1950s and early 1960s some of the local businesses closed. The marker tells us, "Eventually leaving only the post office and two churches." Much later than most mill owners, they sold the homes to the residents in 1966.

"WHAT'S THE DIFFERENCE BETWEEN Acworth and Clarkdale Thread Mills?" That was the title of a *Marietta Daily Journal* article on November 18, 1954. It can be confusing when you consider there were two Coats and Clark Mills in Cobb County. Coats and Clark came to Georgia to buy the Acworth Hosiery Mill and later built Clarkdale, village and all. Georgia has other mills in Toccoa. In honor of the Clark family, the name of the town of Austell was changed to Clarkdale. Over the next twenty years, mills were added in Toccoa (1937), Pelham (1943), Albany (1947) and Thomasville (1947). The *Daily Journal* article described the Acworth thread mill as having Egyptian cotton that was soft and silky, blended ten times and then doubly blended before being "bloomed to make it fluffy." From one end to the other, bales of cotton become thread. The cotton was finally made into a "lap," or a roll of fifty-seven yards at fifty-two pounds each. The taps were "carded, combed and made into thread." More than thirty thousand pounds of unfinished three-ply thread were produced each week at the Acworth Mill in 1954. The only difference between Acworth and Clarkdale Mill was that the latter was larger and produced more thread.[91]

Residents' Voices

Clarkdale was a safe mill village. Raymond Meadows worked at Coats and Clark and never had to lock the doors. Meadows said, "You just left it open. People wouldn't come and you wouldn't have trouble from anybody."

The mill hired entire families. "Back then, you know, they were happy to have the families working here," Meadows said. "They didn't say, 'Your granddaddy worked here, you can't work here'…in fact, all three of my brothers worked here."

Like Meadows, Bill Maxwell grew up in the Clarkdale village, with many family members working in the mill. He worked summers, but his aunt and grandparents had jobs at Coats and Clark. He shared about his grandparents struggling to make it on the family farm: "So when the mill opened, they headed down this way to go to work at the mill because it was just easier than trying to farm every year, if you're having bad luck or something, and you lived in a nice little house that was provided for you for a nominal rent—that's why they came down here."[92]

"You know Rosie the Riveter? Well, I was one of them," said Rachel Simpson Casey Holt, who spent thirty-seven years at the thread mill. She worked at the Marietta Bell Bomber Plant and then was laid off. Holt said there were few places for "people like her who didn't have an education."

Lillian Fainn started working at the Coats and Clark mill in 1973 and remembered her first day. "It was loud in here; we had to wear earplugs. The first day I thought, 'Am I going to be able to do this?' But then you get used to it."

She had to work. She had a six-month-old and three other children at home. She worked for ten years running sides and changing travelers. She explained that these were the metal clips that guided thread into a bobbing. When they wore out, they cut the thread. She recalled working at Clarkdale with fondness: "I don't think I ever missed a day in those ten years. You always wanted to come to work; it was an enjoyable job. We worked hard. It was hard, but we got paid." She remembered it being a happy place to live and work.

The people took care of one another. Fainn said, "If anyone had any problems or they got behind on their bills, everybody pitched in, give them money and stuff like that. Kids that needed clothes, we'd bring them stuff." When Fainn found out that the Clarkdale mill was going to close, she said she "cried all the way home."[93]

The old mill sat silent for years after it closed in the 1980s. In 2001, Austell reclaimed the building. Now the multiuse space is home to city, county and state offices. A paperboard company has leased the entire third floor.[94]

In 2017, the Clarkdale Community Center burned to the ground. For ninety years, the center was the location of neighborhood events. The wooden structure burned quickly, but in 2018, the Cobb commissioners voted to replace the building in Austell. The plan is to include walking trails, playground equipment and a fenced-in dog park. The goal was to build a scaled-down version with many of the same features inside. The plan was created with input from the Clarkdale residents.[95]

ROSWELL

Roswell Mills, 1839

As Adeline walked toward the mill to start her shift, she noticed the unusual quiet. So many of the supervisors were gone, leaving the community empty. She went to the machine and began another long, hot day at Roswell Mills. She was not the only one lost in daydreams.

Georgiana Morgan, young widow and mother of two, was on her job at the woolen mill at Roswell. As she made "Roswell Gray," the material used to sew into Confederate uniforms, Georgiana was thinking about her husband. She wondered if he had been wearing the same gray wool for his uniform when he was buried in Mississippi the year before. Her thoughts were rudely interrupted as men with a Northern twang started shouting orders.

"Get up and go home. Gather up everything you can carry including your children and come back here in two hours. You are all under arrest for treason by the authority of General William Tecumseh Sherman of the Army of the Potomac." Brigadier General Kenner Garrard's cavalry had begun its twelve-day occupation of Roswell and began preparing the "prisoners" for travel to the Marietta Square.

Sherman was clear about his orders: mill owners and employees were to be arrested and charged with treason, an action that puzzles historians to this day. He said:

> *I repeat my orders that you arrest all people, male and female connected with those factories, no matter what the clamor, and let them foot it, under guard, to Marietta, whence I will send them by* [railroad] *cars, to the North....Let them* [the women] *take along their children and clothing, providing they have a means of hauling or you can spare them.*

The owners had fled south to escape the Union occupation. The owners knew it was coming; the workers did not. They left their workers behind.

Sherman thought Garrard was weak and slow, and it was confirmed that he put the women and children on wagons instead of making them walk to Marietta waiting for trains north. Sherman had little compassion for these women and children. He may have been angered by the ruse of the owners to fly a French flag over the woolen mill in hopes the mill would not be burned. Sherman took out his anger on the innocent. He never wrote to his wife about this part of the march through Georgia. He mentioned it in his memoirs as if he were helping these women and children go north. He did not record the truth.

More than four hundred women and their children, and a few men who were too young or too old to fight, were sent by wagon to Marietta and then imprisoned in the abandoned Georgia Military Institute. Some locals paid a fee to have some of the women stay in Marietta to work instead of shipping them north. Some women were raped and mistreated en route to the North.[96]

Adeline and Georgiana were startled from a daydream and walked toward a nightmare. They were herded into suffocating hot trains like cattle. They did not know they were headed for a Northern prisoner of war camp. As the North Georgia mountains grew and then subsided in her view, Georgiana could not know that she was never to see Georgia again. She was punished for doing her job, making cloth at Roswell.

They went north to Chattanooga, Tennessee, and then had a stopover in Nashville. The destination for most was a refugee hospital in Louisville. Later, the women took menial jobs and found somewhere to live. If they were alone or with their children, it was unlikely they would ever make it back to North Georgia. Sherman's only concern was that they were no longer supplying cloth to the enemy. He really did not care what they did after he dropped them off north. They were the lucky ones in Kentucky. Others were just sent over the Ohio River to Indiana. Some found work in a Northern mill. Most could never make enough money to return to the South.

Adeline, who was with child, made her way to Chicago and delivered Mary Ann in August 1864. Not having heard from her husband, she assumed he was dead. Over the next five years, Adeline and her children made their way home to Georgia, mostly on foot. Adeline's return was a surprise to her husband, Joshua. Thinking Adeline herself was dead, he had remarried. Joshua had another surprise coming as well: Adeline had given birth to a son, John Henry, in 1867.

It is not clear how Adeline became pregnant. Perhaps Joshua had found her in Chicago, but that does not explain the new wife or, in the end, what happened to the new wife. Joshua and Adeline were buried together. Baby John Henry must have been accepted by Joshua as his son, but he lived a short life, dying at fifteen. Mary Ann lived until she was eighty-eight. There is no mention of her other children, who were forced north in July 1864. Her simple grave monument has a powerful message: "Roswell Mill Worker Caught and Exiled to Chicago by Yankee Army 1864—Returned on Foot 1869."[97]

Georgiana never returned home to Georgia. In Petite's *The Women Will Howl*, we read, "Nineteen-year-old Georgiana Morgan, her four-year-old son, William and two-year-old daughter Lula were sent north with the workers from Roswell. Georgiana had gone to work in Roswell factories after her husband, Alexander, enlisted in the 42nd Georgia Infantry. Alexander died in Mississippi in July 1863, one year before her arrest. Widowed with two young children and no means of support, Georgiana made her way to Cannelton and found work in the Indiana cotton mill."[98]

The Roswell Mill was rebuilt and changed owners many times. As if cursed, the building burned again in 1926 from a lightning strike. In 1947, the building was purchased by Southern Mills. As cotton production became outsourced in the mid-1970s, the age of King Cotton passed.

Today, the only complete building of the original Roswell Mills is the mechanics shop—a small old brick square building. The historic Roswell Mills area is under the jurisdiction of the U.S. National Park Service and part of the Chattahoochee River Recreation Area.

A ten-foot monument devoted to these hidden figures of the Civil War stands to teach and help Georgians to never forget these millworkers who were arrested and called traitors for doing their job. In July 2000, the Roswell Mills Camp No. 1547, Sons of Confederate Veterans, unveiled the crumbling Corinthian column near the mill site with the inscription:

Honoring the memory of the four hundred women, children, and men mill workers of Roswell who were charged with treason and deported by train to the North by invading Federal Forces.[99]

CHAPTER 6

Douglas County

DOUGLASVILLE

Lois/Beaver Mills, 1908

Douglas County did not exist until 1870. Until that time, the 291-square-mile area was part of Campbell County. During this period of Reconstruction, African Americans were serving in the Georgia legislature. They gave the county a new name in honor of abolitionist Frederick Douglass. The name would not stick, as the Democrats kicked the Reconstructionist out and regained power. They won this battle by dropping the extra *s* and naming the county after Stephen A. Douglas, the Illinois senator who lost the presidency to Abraham Lincoln.[100]

New Manchester was part of a remote section of Campbell County, but Beaver-Lois came later and was always in downtown Douglasville.

As the railroad came to most southern towns, textile industries exploded, bringing work and homes for the workers. In 1895, New Eden Mill was the first in Douglasville. It burned soon after it opened. After a series of failed attempts, the Lois Mill opened in 1908.

Charles Paray's mill design for the exterior walls allowed more light and air into the mill. The walls were called "zig zagged." You can see an example of this in Rome's Celanese/Tubize mill. The building still exists. The Douglas mill no longer exists.

Number 6354 Cooper Street, one of the eighty-eight original mill homes built by Douglasville's Lois-Beaver Mills in 1897. *Library of Congress.*

For easier repair in case of a fire, two foundations were poured. The mill built small-frame houses along Cooper and Grady Streets. These are the remains of the mill village.

In the 1930s, Beaver Mills moved from Massachusetts to buy Lois Mill. Beaver-Lois produced seventeen tons of cotton products each week for clothing production. Most of the broadcloth (90 percent) was sent to other Beaver Mills outside Georgia. The Georgia Western Railroad made Douglas County a major textile shipping community.

While many mills closer to Atlanta tried to unionize, Beaver-Lois mills succeeded in 1933. The workers participated in the 1934 General Textile Strike and closed the mill for four weeks. It was not a success. When the mill reopened, they had more work and less pay. The unrest continued until the mill finally closed in the 1940s. A fire removed any trace of this Douglasville mill in 2012.[101]

New Manchester Mills, 1849

Synthia Catherine Stewart Boyd sat down with her grandson in 1947 and recorded her story with remarkable detail. "I was seven years old when the Civil War began," remembered Synthia at age ninety-two. She was ten years old when the Yankees arrested the millworkers and children in July 1864. There is some confusion from her interview and other records on whether she was captured in Roswell or in New Manchester. This is not a large problem because both mills were invaded and workers arrested and sent on the same trains north. The only difference is that New Manchester Mills were not burned.

Synthia's father, Walter Stewart, was a former mill boss at the New Manchester Mills. He joined the Confederate army in 1862, and after several battles, he was captured and sent to a prisoner of war camp in Ohio. Synthia said, "A friend of Pa's rode up to camp to tell Pa that his baby boy, Jeff Davis, had died. He could come home to the funeral but was ordered back to camp to fight at Kennesaw. Later, in Atlanta, he was taken prisoner and sent north to the infamous Camp Chase in Ohio." In the meantime, his wife and children suffered their own imprisonment.

Synthia expressed horror at being shipped north on a troop train packed with other mill women and children. While some reported getting food rations, Synthia said they had nothing—only the clothing they wore. Most were imprisoned or abandoned in Louisville, Kentucky.

After Stewart's release, he went looking for his family. He discovered that his wife and children had been deported to Louisville, Kentucky, and he found them there. He worked in a local tannery until he earned enough money to get back to Georgia. Most women were not so lucky. With a husband to help provide, some found their way home. Synthia said it best herself: "Some mill women died, some remarried, others were able to save enough to return home. But most were not as fortunate as we were."[102]

Newspapers, both Northern and Southern, condemned Sherman's treatment of the women who were just doing their jobs to make money to feed their kids. They were not traitors. Later, the U.S. government reprimanded Sherman for "issuing calloused and degrading orders against these poor, defenseless mill women."[103]

Today, the three-story New Manchester Mills complex stands hollow, un-torched by Sherman's flames. In Sweetwater Creek State Park in Lithia Springs, Georgia, you can hike to the location and listen for the sounds of the workers. Maybe you will see an apparition or, as the word origin suggests, an "unclosing" of heaven—vaporous wisps of women and children working in the mill, just as they were before they were deported north. Maybe the heavens have opened, and these workers have finally returned home.

CHAPTER 7

Floyd County

LINDALE

Massachusetts Mills/Pepperell/West Point Pepperell, 1897

Everyone's voice is unique. Some speak with authority and others from experience. The following three voices examine life in Lindale. Two men and one boy, all three tied to the mill, tell us their stories.

First to speak is Captain H.P. Meikleham, the Massachusetts Mills agent. Meikleham testified to the U.S. Commission on Industrial Relations in 1915 about labor relations. He defended the mill village conditions at Lindale and testified about his provision for his people.

Norman Hall speaks without words. Lewis Hine photographed Hall in 1913, and the photo speaks. The wrinkled boy was on his way for his shift in the mill. He had finished his education at first grade. Hine, a social reformer, said, "If I could tell the story in words, I wouldn't need to lug around a camera." Norman's image is worth a thousand unspoken words, and yet we hear him.

Wilson Hicks tells us the final story in his own words. He teaches by example and through the journal he left showing how he created opportunities through experiential and formal education. Hicks spent most of his life in Lindale; while gone for a time, he always returned. All the while, Wilson was learning.

Oh Captain! My Captain!: H.P. Meikleham

It was a cool March day in 1915 when Captain Meikleham began his testimony. The 1914 Fulton Bag and Cotton Mill Strike brought the U.S. Commission on Industrial Relations to Atlanta. Its members interviewed witnesses about mill conditions. Investigators Alexander Daly and Inis Weed cross-examined Lindale's leader H.P. Meikleham. Oscar Elsas and Meikleham had corresponded on many issues. Allegedly, the two mill agents colluded on labor issues.

Captain Henry Parish Meikleham was the agent at the Lindale Mill from 1899 until his death in 1937. *Eleanor Hicks Popham and family.*

April Longworth wrote, "Southern Democrats and local business owners joined together to make the investigation at the Fulton Bag and Cotton Mill as ineffectual as possible, while undermining the authority of the U.S. Commission on Industrial Relations."[104] Before Daly and Weed left town, Lindale's Captain had testified:

> *"Mr. H.P. Meikleham, you have been sworn in.* [Alexander Daly begins his examination.] *Mr. Meikleham, what is your official position?"*
> *"Agent of the Massachusetts Mill in Georgia, at Lindale."*
> *"How long have you been such agent?"*
> *"Fifteen years."*
> *"What are your duties as agent?"*
> *"I am the general manager of the Mill and local representative of the Treasurer."*
> *"How many people are employed in your Mill?"*
> *"About, on the average, 1500."*
> *"Have you in mind the number of men, women and children employed separately?"*
> *"Before the last law went into effect, January 1st 1915, all children under the age of fifteen years have been eliminated from the Mill. Today we have about 850 males and about 650 females."*

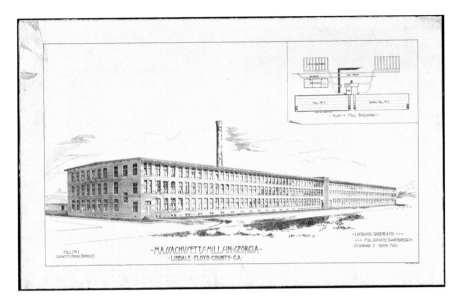

Above: Building plans
for the Lindale Mills,
with a thirty-thousand-
spindle capacity. *Rome
Area History Museum*.

Right: Artist's rendering
of Lindale Mills. *Rome
History Museum*.

The interrogation continued, and Meikleham explained that Lindale has 3,200 residents and that the mill sits on about one thousand acres, all of it within the city limits. This includes the mill village homes provided by the mill. He further explained that the mill has no jurisdiction over the unincorporated town of Lindale. He noted that they did not have interest in the local businesses in the town, but they rented the Mill Store building.

Daly moved to question Meikleham about mill conditions at Lindale:

"Are you familiar with the working conditions, the relations that exist between the mill and your labor?"

"Yes, Sir."

"Have you ever had any labor troubles in the mill?"

"Never…with one exception. About ten years ago a few of the loom fixers then in the Mills stated they would quit if they did not have more pay."

"How was that adjusted?"

"By discharging the dissatisfied loom fixers."

"What procedure is followed in your mill when any dispute arises with some one or more employees? What remedy does he have in order that any dispute that may be adjudicated?"

Meikleham explained the company policy and procedure: "He takes his dispute up to the overseer of his department. If he is not satisfied with the adjustment he can appeal to the superintendent or myself, who reserve the hours from twelve to twelve forty-five for all such questions, when the help have free access to us."

Daly questioned, "And you are the final judge?" Meikleham replied, "I am the final judge in labor." Daly then moved on to the mill homes provided by the company:

"Are the houses built of one certain size, or are they of different sizes?"

"They are single house. They are single houses of five or six rooms and double houses of from six to twelve rooms."

"Have you any rules and regulations as to how many families may live in one house?"

"No, Sir."

"Do more than one family live in one house?"

"I don't think so, except relations."

"In these double houses how many people on an average, would inhabit them?

"I should say it would run hardly one person to the room."

"Are those houses furnished free to the operatives, or do they pay rent for them?"

"They pay rent."

"Are they charged by the room or by the month, or by the week, or how?"

"By the room per week."

"What would be the average?"

"The average is 25 cents per room each week."

"Do you know what the cost of building such house is?"

"I have just asked for a bid for five houses of eight rooms each, and it has been $150 per room. We have built some cheaper and some that have cost more."

"What sanitary arrangements are there in them if any?"

"A number of the houses have baths and closets, mostly for overseers, second hands, clerks, railway officials, and ministers."

"What are the sanitary arrangements of the houses you speak about that rent for 25 cents per room?"

"After a great deal of study and investigation we have adopted what they call the Durham English System. They are large wood houses behind each house and in there is a toilet and tub underneath that is emptied twice a week and disinfected from two to four times a week. The contents of these tubs are buried."

Daly wanted to know if there was a sewer system in Lindale. The Lindale agent answered vaguely:

"Yes Sir, but not in general."

"Where do those operatives obtain their water supply?"

"They use a pump to the reservoir, and is thrown by gravity over the houses."

"Is there a system of filtration connected with the reservoir or not?"

"No Sir, the springs are protected and the water is analyzed from two to four times a year by the Boston, Massachusetts Institute of Technology."

"Have you had any epidemics in the village for any length of time past?"

"About six years ago we had an epidemic of typhoid. About fourteen years ago we had an epidemic of small pox but this was prevalent all though the Southern country."

The interrogator continued:

> *"Have you seen any cases of pellagra in your mill village?"*
>
> *"Yes, Sir."* [Daly examined the number of cases and questioned Meikleham about the food supply, leading up to another concern.]
>
> *"Were the cases of pellagra among employees that have been employed for a long period of time or some reasonable period of time, or from the floating population that may have gone through your plant?"*
>
> *"I do not know, but I should say it would be about half and half."*
>
> *"You have a doctor there?"*
>
> *"Yes Sir, three physicians."*
>
> *"Are they employed at the mill?"*
>
> *"One is employed by the mill to supervise the help of the village and attend to all injuries, accidents, and look after the health of any people that were sent to him."*
>
> *"Are their services free?"*
>
> *"Their services are free to all where it is necessary."*
>
> *"Are there any deductions from their wages?"*
>
> *"No, Sir."*

Daly questioned him about hospital facilities, and Meikleham told him about the room for accidents and the first-aid kit. Meikleham was asked about the school in town, and he explained that it is on mill property—they pay for three months of school, and the county pays for five months. This allows the children eight months of school until the eighth grade. He explained that all the teachers are required to visit all the homes of his workers several times per year. He admitted they have tried night school but had few takers:

> *"Are the children required to attend?"*
>
> *"No Sir, only as far as we can get them to attend."*
>
> *"Who attends to that?"*
>
> *"I do."*

Daly wondered if the parents pushed their kids to go to school. Meikleham replied, "Not as they should, but it is growing every year. The average attendance is 300 and the total enrollment is 600."

Daly wanted to know about the transient population working in his mills for short periods. Meikleham explained, "The main reason is that they stay in

Photographer Lewis Hine wrote, "Noon hour at Massachusetts Mills, Lindale, Ga. During the days following this, I proved the ages of nearly a dozen of these children, by gaining access to Family Records, Insurance papers, and through conversations with the children and parents, and found these that I could prove to be working now, or during the past year at 10 and 11 years of age, some of them having begun before they were ten. Further search would reveal dozens or more." *Library of Congress.*

one place until they have obtained all the credit they own at the stores and then move to establish fresh credit somewhere else; and the other reason is that there is a certain number that is always trying another mill to see if they do not like it better."

The interrogation then changed focus to the people of the mill. Meikleham explained that many of his workers came from the hill country and off the farms; they came with disease and malnourishment:

> *"They are anemic and very emaciated and stooped over. After a period of time, they looked like entirely different people. They improved very rapidly morally, mentally, physically and every other way."*
>
> *"Are they saving, frugal people?"*
>
> *"Hardly any of them. I started a savings department about twelve years ago. I got as high as 20,000 in deposits, mainly by the overseers and more intelligent class. The savings department today has gone down to about 6,000 with not over one dozen depositors. I am going to cut it out this year owing to lack of interest."*

Meikleham explained that few owned their own homes and fewer family members were working in the mill. Where the whole family used to work, now only one or two worked in the mill. And "the younger members drop out."

An interesting back and forth between Daly and Meikleham led to livestock. Daly asked if his mill villagers had room for grazing and asked him if the mill would help them purchase a cow. Meikleham noted that the mill would and would take it out of their paycheck.

Daly examined Meikleham's relationship with his workers:

"What contact do you have with people in the mill?"

"I know them everyone by name. My relations are close with them."

"What effect has this close personal relationship that you have with your help upon the operation and conditions in your mill and the success that you have had in your business, if any?"

"It makes us all one big family, and without bragging, I consider it one of the most successful mills I have ever known and it has caused the help to come in and back me up to the fullest extent as a matter of pride and loyalty to make better work and more work. It is the strongest esprit de corps *that I have ever known. There are two things necessary; one is to be fair, and the other is to be straight and loyal with them and you can accomplish results that cannot be accomplished in any other way…*

"You have got to get their loyalty and when you have got it, they will make a success; I don't care who they are. To these conditions I attribute the fact that outside influences find it impossible to go in there and accomplish any results, they confide their trouble to me nearly every time…

"In the event of a loose character, male or female finding their way into the community, the same is immediately reported to me by anyone or by quite a number of the employees with the demand that such persons be instantly notified to get out of town. I consider them the most moral people that I have come in contact with. I'll bet you a thing cannot happen in Lindale in 24 hours that I won't know the truth of it. I know every person that is gambling; and I know every person that is fooling with liquor. I might not be able to get the proof to convict them, but the fellow that is selling booze will and tell me is he selling booze, and if I don't bother him, he will tell me everything."

Daly returned to the conditions of the mill and the village:

"What sanitary condition have you in the mill?"
"We have a number of toilets each, for males and females properly separated, with washroom attachment and these toilets are all enamel brick and steel, and even the seats, and they are washed every night with hose from top to bottom and thoroughly disinfected. The disinfecting is carried to such an extent that the whole village is sprayed with Chloro-naptholeum twice a week, a big cart come down with hose connections and sprays the whole town. During the two years I have done it you cannot find a fly in that town."[105]

H.P. Meikleham managed the mill and Lindale for more than forty years. He was the perfect prototype of the paternalist mill manager. Local attorney Barry Wright spoke of Meikleham on August 1, 1937: "When he came here he found a new, ugly place, with bare unfinished grounds, with a little grass, flowers or shrubbery, and with hardly a tree. He found a small failing mill, unsuccessful almost to failing, and the people who worked here confronted by uncertainty." He continued to praise Meikleham and his work at Lindale for the Lindale Bible Class:

He was still in his twenties, with the body and energies of an athlete, and he gave everything he had to building, changing, and improving, not only the mill which was a source of livelihood, but the houses, the village, and the lives of the people.
In only a few years, a struggling mill had expanded to one of the largest in the country; successful management had insured continued operation and steady employment; contentment had followed uncertainty, and Lindale, the pride of his heart, became known far and near as a good place to live and work, the home of a people universally respected for their character.[106]

The Captain and the Mill

Early in the twentieth century, under Captain Meikleham, Lindale was booming. As production grew in the Lindale Mill, so did the need for workers. The mill built more homes. The mill hired families with the most children able to work. This paternalism was a growing trend. Mill communities throughout the county provided nonwage benefits to encourage corporate community. Lindale was no exception.

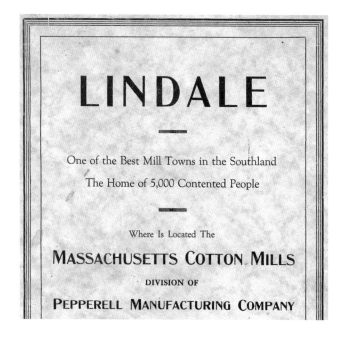

LINDALE

One of the Best Mill Towns in the Southland

The Home of 5,000 Contented People

Where Is Located The

MASSACHUSETTS COTTON MILLS

DIVISION OF

PEPPERELL MANUFACTURING COMPANY

The 1939 Lindale Mills booklet, with history and events, touted "The Home of 5000 Contented People" and the best mill in the south. *Popham family.*

The company provided qualified and well-paid grade school teachers. By 1932, they had built a free kindergarten. The mill offered night school with transfer credits to Georgia Technical Institute. According to Meikleham, few took advantage. The elementary school packed classrooms with children of large families still too young to enter the plant.

Healthcare was guaranteed in Lindale. Doctors were on staff and made house calls. A nurse lived in Lindale, and someone was on call all day, seven days a week. There was also a town dentist. The goal was to keep the workers healthy and productive.

In the early part of the century, the walk or even a buggy ride to Rome was an ordeal. So, Lindale had two department stores. Workers could use credit with payroll deductions. Grocery stores, milk, egg, butter and vegetable deliveries made Lindale a self-contained community. The company provided many of these nonwage benefits to keep the operative close to home. This paternalist system required a leader. So, to lead them, or to control them, Harry Parris Meikleham became "the Captain."

H.P. Meikleham was the mill agent or plant manager from 1899 to 1937. According to his own testimony, the Captain would have known Norman Hall. Norman enjoyed the Christmas traditions started by Meikleham. He started a tradition in 1933 that continues today. One week before Christmas, Meikleham ordered workers to build a five-pointed wooden star. The "Mill Star" was twelve feet across and covered with tin. A crew hoisted the three-hundred-pound, light-encrusted star between the 250-foot smokestacks. Every year since 1933, Christmas is remembered in Lindale. The star commissioned by Meikleham has been replaced with a much lighter version. The weakened stacks can longer support the original.

The Captain started many of the other Christmas traditions that exist to this day in Lindale. He used to say, "This is *our* Christmas." Some felt that he was creating community, while others felt it was a way of controlling the millworkers. Daniel Scott Wilson grew up in Lindale and remembered the holidays: "Nothing happened in Lindale…that did not benefit the company." This was a subtle example of corporate paternalism. Wilson continued:

> *I have found that most of the Christmas holidays as celebrated at Lindale served to help the company and not necessarily the people. Christmas in the cotton mill village was intended to keep the people under management's control. Paternalism created my Christmas. And it starts with the Christmas Star.*[107]

The Captain may have created the Mill Star for more reasons than holiday cheer. In 1933, President Franklin Delano Roosevelt created the National Industrial Recovery Act (NIRA). This New Deal plan was to force prosperous industries to close one week out of the month. This gave the suffering mills a chance to catch up. But this also forced Lindale to shut down and cut employee wages. Things got tight for the Lindale employees, especially at Christmas. The Captain may have had the star placed to foster community and good will. It worked.

Loyalty was important to Lindale workers. In 1934, textile workers across the South revolted against malicious mill owners. Lindale did not revolt. Instead, the workers wanted management to save them from the evil federal government. Lindale Mill workers felt protected during the Great Depression. In 1935, the U.S. Supreme Court struck down the NIRA.

Wilson said, "The star was a symbol of hope for the employees to look toward during the hard times of the Great Depression. He hoped the star would draw people to the village—just as the star brought the three wise men to the birthplace of Jesus." The Captain may have seen it as another way to manage the lives of the operatives in Lindale.[108]

One young man was likely influenced, in some way, by the Captain. His image, taken by Lewis Hine, in the 1900s is haunting.

The Wrinkled Boy: Norman Hall

Norman walked with dread toward the stacks. Each step took him away from his mill home on Park Avenue in Lindale and away from school—his only way out of the mill. Each reluctant stride took this ten-year-old wrinkled boy to work. Work was the lint-choked spinning floor of the Massachusetts Mills. On this bright April day in 1913, Norman noticed a commotion. Outside the mill gate, a man stood out of place. The bespectacled man was taking pictures and notes. Lewis Hine was busy setting up his tripod camera when Norman walked by. His eyes focused downward when Hine called out to him.

"Can I take your picture?" Hine asked. Norman looked up. Hine knew he did not have the words to tell this boy's story when he looked in his disheveled eyes. Hine would have to let his camera lens do its job.

Norman was dirty before he got to work and the sun was hurting his eyes, so he squinted as Lewis Hine focused his camera. The explosion of the ancient camera froze Norman Hall in time—dirt and all. The dirt lines highlighted the lines on his face that belonged to a middle-aged man, not a ten-year-old boy. Hine asked Norman his name and age, and Norman replied, "Norman Hall, and I'm twelve," according to Russell's *Lost Towns of North Georgia*. Hine expected the standard lie and made a mental note to check the insurance papers. Hine could measure the height of a child by the buttons on his vest and determine their age. He also could talk his way into the mill office and the mill floor.

Norman told Hine that his father and brothers also worked in the plant and that he wanted to contribute. He said, "My parents said work never hurt a kid, and I want to do my part. Plus, we get to live in the company mill house, if we all work there."

Lewis Hine not only photographed the children who worked in the mill but also captured the mill homes. He would comment about the housing conditions, "Not a thing neglected, except the child."

Hine's images would shock the nation and force Congress to act. In 1913, he worked with the National Child Labor Committee (NCLC) to show the images to Congress. This led to solid legislation in 1938. The government began enforcing strict child labor laws.[109]

Norman did not need to speak. His picture did all the talking for him. His image reveals a time when the whole family worked in the mill. Despite Captain Meikleham's 1915 testimony, entire families were still working in the mill. Children were in the mills until the 1930s, when the government enforced new child labor laws.

Left: Norman Hall, young doffer, at Massachusetts Mills in Lindale Mills. Lewis Hine, photographer. *Library of Congress.*

Right: Luther Dories was a doffer in Spinning Room no. 2, Massachusetts Mills, Lindale, Georgia. Photographer Hines commented, "Said 12 years old, but very doubtful. Father and brother work." Hines suggested that Luther did not need to work. April 1913. *Library of Congress.*

Norman worked in the textile mills his entire life. He moved to the Goodyear plant (Atco) in Bartow County and worked as a doffer. He was a veteran of World War I and enlisted in World War II at the age of forty-one. His military enlistment card revealed his first-grade education. He signed an "X" because he could not read or write. He died in 1962, and alongside his wife, Eva, his gravestone reads, "Norman M. Hall Gone but Not Forgotten."

Norman did not have a chance. He lived a tough, hardworking life, but he paved the way for children who came behind him in the mills. His image (along with many others) stopped other young children having to work in the mills. It took some time, but the New Deal got children out of the Lindale Mill. Children like Wilson Hicks benefited. Although he wanted to work in the Lindale Mills before he was sixteen, he had to leave. Wilson Hicks had a better life than Norman Hall.

Education Matters: Wilson Hicks

Joseph Wilson Hicks started at Lindale before he was sixteen years old. He was forced to leave when the National Recovery Act (NRA) regulated child labor laws. He returned to live and work in Lindale until he retired. *Eleanor Hicks Popham and family.*

Joseph Wilson Hicks started to work in the Massachusetts Mills in Lindale before he was sixteen years old. He left a short memoir for his family. In it, Hicks wrote about how excited he was to work in the mill, but he had to leave because the law changed. He had to wait until he was sixteen.[110]

Wilson was born in 1918 in Crystal Springs, in a rural section of Floyd County. His father, a road contractor, was killed on the job when Wilson was only four years old. They moved to the textile town of Lindale. Wilson started school in Lindale but moved to Florida with his family.

In 1926, a hurricane destroyed his Florida home. He wrote, "I remember Mother holding my hand as we went out of the house, just as it was blown off the foundation.…The wind was terrific. I saw chairs, cups, etc., blowing through the air like small pieces of paper. We held to deep rooted bushes to keep from being blown away." He concluded, "Soon after the hurricane we gathered up the things we could salvage and came back to Lindale."[111]

Wilson completed eighth grade in Lindale. His school was in the basement of Lindale Auditorium. While he was in school, he earned money by shining shoes in front of the company store on the weekends. He quit school in 1933. He wanted to work in the textile mill when he was fourteen. Wilson felt like he needed to make his own living at this young age. His first job was sweeping the spinning room floor. Wilson recalled, "It did not last long because the eight-hour law was passed, and I had to wait until I was sixteen before I could go back to work."

When Wilson turned sixteen, he returned to the textile mill in the beamer room. After several jobs, the mill laid him off. Wilson said, "I was very lucky, I was never fired from any job, just laid off."

The mill shut down many times, and Wilson had to find other work. Finally, he returned to the mill, where he had to train and retrain for new jobs. He was always learning. He worked any shift to try to get ahead, as he was a newlywed hoping to "start keeping house."

While working on his regular job, he asked the overseer's permission to learn to grind cards. To make it legit, the supervisor gave him a card oiling job. This allowed Hicks time to work with the experienced card grinder. Wilson said, "The oiling job was my first promotion and I was really happy."[112] After only a few weeks, Wilson caught a break. He filled in for the second shift card grinders, as he was on jury duty when the foreman asked him to set up the rollers. The supervisor liked his work and asked him to come to first shift to grind. But it did not work out.

The company gave the job to another worker who had one more year of textile school. Wilson was not angry; he recognized the importance of training. He knew that at the right time, he would want the mill to acknowledge his time in textile school. Three weeks later, the overseer told Wilson to report to first shift. He received a pay raise and began learning everything about his job and other jobs. They had finally moved into the mill village. Wilson said, "Mickey and I were on cloud nine."[113]

He kept learning. He said, "During this time, I continued my textile schooling and eventually earned a Carding Diploma plus credits for Spinning and Weaving."[114] The more he learned, the more his pay increased. He was able to get into a three-room apartment on Walnut Street in Lindale. It was just in time, as Wilson and Mickey had brought Eleanor Jo into the world in 1942. And then came the war. Hicks asked to enlist, but the company wanted him to defer. He refused and joined the Merchant Marines.

Mickey Hicks worked as a nursing assistant in the Lindale Mills clinic. *Eleanor Hicks Popham and family.*

He did not have a high school diploma and went in as a mess man, third class, but that changed. Wilson said, "I studied really hard and made grades in the upper third of my classes. Due to my grades, I was offered radio training in Sheepshead Bay, New York. I turned this down and took deck training graduating in the upper third of the class as an Ordinary Seaman. The War ended while I was in training." Discharged on December

23, 1946, he arrived in Lindale on Christmas Eve with gifts in hand. He brought a beautiful doll and ball for his daughter, Eleanor. Wilson said, "Soon after Christmas, we returned to our house on Walnut Street and began to live again."[115]

He returned to his old job as a card overhauler, but the mills had plans for him to be a foreman. He knew he had to get his high school diploma. He started classes at Rome High School. After three weeks, the teacher asked him where he had attended textile classes. She inquired about his Merchant Marine training. She told him to come the next night, and she gave him a test. He did not need any more classes—Wilson had tested at a college level. He took the high school equivalency at Rome High School, and in two weeks, he had a diploma in hand. The education of Wilson Hicks did not stop there.

He took correspondence courses in mechanical engineering. In January 1948, the mill promoted Wilson to foreman. This promotion meant straight time and more benefits. This helped with growing family issues of caring for sick loved ones. One year later, the bosses moved him to first shift. Wilson said, "This was the highlight of my life. I was in seventh heaven."[116]

Wilson bought his first new car. Then the mill gave him a home in the Jamestown section of Lindale at 3 South Terrace Avenue. His daughter, Eleanor Jo, remembered growing up in the mill village. She did not feel controlled by the Captain or the mill. Miss Ellie said, "It was a wonderful place to grow up. Everybody's parents took care of all the kids in the village. Never afraid of anything, [we] always felt safe."[117] Ellie described how the company took care of the homes by painting and fixing the plumbing. At some point, the mill sold the mill houses to the renters.

Life was easier for Wilson, so he became active in the Lindale Lodge and became a community leader. With a group of other residents, Wilson started the Floyd County Wildlife Association and later became the president. He was very proud of his work of founding the wildlife association.

Wilson worked at Lindale for most of his adult life. He was the president of the Quarter Century Club, a group for employees of the textile mill with twenty-five years of service. In the late 1960s, opportunity knocked and Wilson left Lindale. In the 1970s, he worked in a Cartersville plant. However, when he had the chance, he came back to Lindale, now Pepperell Mills, to be an auditor and then a foreman. He came home. Wilson Hicks retired on February 25, 1981.

While he enjoyed retirement, he kept on learning. Wilson went to various textile schools throughout his career. He had many certificates for course

Pepperell employees in training. Technical education was important at Pepperell in Lindale from an early date. After retirement, Wilson (*front row, fourth from left*) continued his education—a Coosa Valley Tech certificate was found in his records. *Eleanor Hicks Popham and family.*

completions. The mill at Lindale encouraged education for advancement. Wilson was working his way up.

Wilson had no idea that his legacy of learning would continue. His daughter, Ellie, would have a son, Kurt, who would marry someone like his grandfather. Wilson valued continuing education. In the late 1990s, Kurt's wife, Heidi, began working at Georgia Northwestern Technical College. As the president's executive assistant, she continued her education. In 2019, Dr. Heidi K. Popham became the president of Georgia Northwestern Technical College. While helping the author research this story, she unearthed an interesting connection. Among Wilson Hicks's records, she discovered another certificate of completion. He had taken a small engines course at Coosa Valley Tech, which is now Georgia Northwestern Technical College. Education matters.

The War Years and Beyond

In 1926, Pepperell Manufacturing Company bought Massachusetts Cotton Mills. Some documents still called the mill "Massachusetts Cotton Mills." The mill paid for Pepperell Junior High School and expanded education through ninth grade. Mill owners encouraged children to stay in school and stay out of the mill. They continued to subsidize teachers' pay.

Built in 1940, the Lindale Auditorium became the social hub of the town. The large multilevel brick and stucco building had a manicured lawn. The auditorium housed a theater, a barbershop, a billiard room and a sandwich shop. The food was cheap. A hamburger was a nickel, and a shake was a dime.

In the basement of the Lindale Auditorium was a tiled and heated swimming pool. It cost a dime to swim. The indoor pool was unusual for the time, and it was the only one in the region.

Sundays saw Bible study in the morning and a movie in the afternoon. Movies were a dime until you were twelve years old, and then the price went up to a quarter. Everyone knew everyone, so you could not cheat your way in and say you were younger than twelve. Sometimes the Lindale Band would play in the afternoon.

Baseball was a favorite pastime in all southern mill towns, and Lindale was no different. Lindale had a top-notch field; other teams preferred the Massachusetts Mill fields. On game day, the mill would close in time for the people to support the Lindale team. The management gave key players Mondays and Fridays off to rest for weekend games.

World War II provided textile contracts keeping the mill running three shifts. Pepperell supplied the armed forces with all the textiles they needed. When men left for war, women took over. The mill honored the veterans when the war was over and remembered their dead. They took care of one another during the war, and the mill town continued to prosper.

Wounded soldiers, while convalescing, came to Lindale Auditorium for Movie Night. A Rome bus ran a route on the weekends. Many wartime romances started on movie night between Lindale women and lonely soldiers.

Southern Railroad had a full-time staff at the Lindale depot. Each day, a train ran from Chattanooga to Atlanta and back again in the evening. Each way, the train stopped in Lindale to deliver mail and parcels. The post office, located in the back of the company store, brought that mail to military wives.

Pepperell Mill Team from 1949

The 1949 Lindale (Pepperell) baseball team. *Rome Area History Center.*

Good feelings about Lindale prevailed. Longtime residents felt that it was a good place to work. The pay was good and the work steady. Billy Atkins and Jim Givens grew up in Lindale during the 1940s and called it "a utopia south of Rome." A 1930s yearbook pronounced on the cover, "One of the best mill towns in the Southland. The home of 5000 contented people."[118]

When the war ended and the men returned home, things began to change in Lindale. The law required that the men returning to the mill should get their jobs back. Many came back, but some did not. Having experienced the world, some men chased new opportunities. The GI Bill allowed families to stop renting the mill homes and move outside Lindale. The road to Rome became populated with GI Bill homes.

Pepperell followed the trend of many of the mill towns and began selling the mill homes to the employees. Most of the employees bought the houses. The mill was no longer responsible for the maintenance of the homes. Neglect crept into the community. That set a series of events in motion.

Soon the company store and the post office closed. The old school closed when the county built another one outside Lindale. Even the beauty shop closed. Southern Railroad stopped its daily runs and demolished the depot.

The former textile league games were no longer played on the company baseball fields. When gas was no longer rationed, people left Lindale to find entertainment. They no longer needed the Lindale Auditorium for their sole place of recreation.

The textile industry changed, and production slowed. When the mill went on "short time," people began to find employment elsewhere and moved away. The loyalty was gone, and paternalism was a thing of the past. The company would no longer be the "father figure." The village began to lose its way.[119]

Denim Saves the Day

He came to shut it down. Richard Wolfe came to Lindale in 1977 to close the mill. West Point Pepperell told him not to move his family because he would not be there long. When Wolfe got to Lindale, he saw potential, not only in the mill but also in the people. At the time, there were 2,200 mill employees.

In 1965, West Point Mills merged with Pepperell. Greenwood Mills then purchased West Point Pepperell in 1986. Richard Wolfe understood the people in Lindale. He grew up in a mill village in LaGrange, Georgia, and was one of them. As the new vice-president, he could not stand the thought putting people out of work. Wolfe made a plan to save the mill by tapping into the burgeoning denim market.

The corporate office took notice and gave Wolfe permission to spend on capital improvements. They changed the plant into a top indigo denim producer, selling 1 million yards per week to top jean makers. By the 1990s, Lindale was a world-class operation. Wolfe went to Venezuela in 1990 to build another denim operation for Greenwood Mills. Then the denim market crashed. Lindale succumbed.

Greenwood Mills cut production in 1999, keeping only the dyeing and finishing departments. Little by little, jobs evaporated. Then, on September 28, 2001, at 3:00 p.m., the final whistle closed the plant for good.

Richard Wolfe had retired in 1996, but he had kept Lindale alive for twenty-five more years. He repurposed the mill and built a market to give the residents years of income. The community honored Wolfe by dedicating a park named for him. The Richard Wolfe Park will provide greenspace in Lindale for generations to come. It remains today across from the crumbling Lindale Mills.[120]

All Is Not Lost

Lindale as a mill village is lost to history. Working-class people still live in the mill homes. The Lindale community tried to save the mill and find a new purpose. Companies have come in and salvaged the textile equipment. Others have repurposed the floors and the bricks. As the building gets smaller, one thing has remained: the community's resolve to restore.

The evidence is all over town, pleading with citizens to "Restore Lindale." The Bartow History Museum restored the original courthouse with wood flooring from the mill. A house in Atlanta used mill bricks from the crumbling walls for its new walls.[121] Many of the homes are still standing—a few fully renovated and well maintained.

In 2010, a Seattle family, Joe and Dani Silva, bought the Lindale Mill. The family intended to demolish the mill and move on. Something or "someone" told them to stop and restore it. The family has reclaimed the twenty-three acres of brick and open spaces, with bridges and dams over the flowing Silver Creek. It is open to movie productions, photography and weddings.[122] Every Christmas, the new and third Lindale Star hangs lit in memorial to times gone by.

ROME

Anchor Duck Mills, 1901

In September 2009, the $2,000 Anchor Duck Mill monument was unveiled on the property of the Floyd County Health Department. Just below the flagpole, the location of the mill was marked long after its demolition.

Anchor Duck opened in 1901 and made broadcloth for awnings, tents and sails. A former employee said the textile mill made tents for the army and upholstery for Ford Motor Company. The company owners tried to incentivize work since there were several other mills in town by offering a mill village with 150 homes and community amenities such as a company store, a meeting hall, a barbershop and a school. A resident remembered Wednesday night movies: "We had a recreation center, and I remember we had free movies there every Wednesday night."[123]

Mike Ragland was a local historian, Georgia author and guest columnist for the *Rome News Tribune*. Before his untimely death, he described Anchor Duck:

Above: Rome, Georgia's Anchor Duck Mills' sewing machine and operator. *Rome History Museum.*

Opposite: Anchor Duck Mills, Office No. 10, Rome, Georgia. This building no longer exists. In 2009, there was a public unveiling of the Anchor Duck Mills memorial monument at the flagpole in front of the Floyd County Health Department on Twelfth Street, where the Anchor Duck Mills once stood. *Hargrett Rare Book and Manuscript Library, University of Georgia.*

As 1901 began, two things happened on the Rome/Floyd County Textile program. The first was Henry Parrish Meikleham took over the Massachusetts Cotton Mill of Georgia in Lindale.

The second thing was that closer to Rome, a handful of local businessmen, opened another textile mill. They acquired a four-acre tract of land between Silver Creek and the Chattanooga, Rome, and Southern railroad.[124]

An early 1900s newspaper clipping about Anchor Duck Mills noted:

The Anchor Duck Mills is a thing of beauty and a pride forever to the loyal Roman who visits this wonderful plant and realizes that it means to Rome veritable "heart throbs" of industrial life. It would take volumes and the language of romance to tell of the phenomenal growth of this institution and the part it plays in the progress and prosperity of Rome.[125]

The mill must have had an early marketing team come up with this over-the-top description of a 1900s textile mill. The mill was smaller than many of the mills in the Rome area. The mill's baseball field was once used to graze village cows.[126] Anchor Duck was involved in the 1934 General Textile Strike and a later strike all its own.

During World War I, Anchor Duck supplied large military contracts but could not keep up with demand. In World War II, workers were given sharp increases in wages due to wage competition with defense-related companies.[127]

Later, the company made car headliners and other automobile upholstery for Ford, its largest contractor.[128] In later years, the mill opened the plant to sell curtain cloth on Wednesdays, as ladies in the community would purchase the cloth.

There was lint in the air that ended up in workers' lungs. The owners went to great expense to fix electric fans that misted fine droplets of water to keep the yarn from breaking. The yarn was taken care of, but the lungs of the workers were not.

In 1948, labor unions came to town, and Anchor participated. The strike lingered for ten months. Friends and neighbors clashed. The camaraderie and good feelings in the Anchor community were tarnished as they went to war with one another. Local newspaper accounts recorded shootings,

Anchor Duck Mills, Rome, Georgia, was a vibrant community off East Twelfth Street. The young adults with with corsages are perhaps mill employees or family members. *Rome History Museum.*

beatings and threats. Large newspaper ads were taken out to promote the workers and unions. The mill owners took out full-page ads extolling the good nature of the mill. The family feelings of mill village life disappeared along with the mill stacks and bricks.[129]

The name changed to Anchor Rome in 1947, when Alabama Mills Corporation purchased Anchor Duck. Dan River was the final owner and final name for the mill. In 1958, Dan River bought the mill to close it and end competition with its Virginia mill.

The village homes were not as well built as some of the other Rome mill villages. The red "Condemned" sign appeared often in the South Rome area. Nothing remains except the monument on Twelfth Street in Rome, placed by former employees. The numbers at the reunions dwindle as time steals them from us.

RIVERSIDE DISTRICT

Celanese/Tubize, 1929

Celanese came late to the game. The manufacturer of Italian rayon came to town in 1929, constructed by American Chatillon Corporation. The company broke ground just north of the Rome city limits in the Riverside District of Floyd County. The company did not want to build a mill village, but workers were not attracted to work in the mills without housing like the other mills in the county. So, the company set out to build the best housing in town. It planned a well-designed and very modern mill village with nearly five hundred brick, shoebox homes. Twenty-five of those homes were for management only. The workers could choose from five different floorplans with three to six rooms. The company also offered cheaper duplexes. All the houses had indoor plumbing and electricity. In the village, Celanese offered a school, a clinic, a general store, a pharmacy and several fire houses.

The company also bought a white frame home across the street that had once been owned by Major Ridge, the Cherokee leader who signed the Treaty of New Echota in 1835. The building was used as a home for the superintendent of the mill. Now it is the site of the Chieftains Museum.

In 1930, Chatillon merged with a Belgian company, Tubize. The company was known as Tubize-Chatillon until after World War II. The British company Celanese Corporation of America bought the village and the mill.

The Celanese Mills village is also known as Riverside. The residents remember that a large pool across from the Chieftains served as the neighborhood pool. They learned how to swim in the cool waters of the mill pool. Rome, Georgia, 2019. *Author's collection.*

These unique ridges in the weaving rooms allowed for more air and light in the mills. Tubize (Celanese), Rome, Georgia, 2019. *Author's collection.*

The mill village would forever be known as Celanese.

Celanese followed other mills with mill villages and in the 1950s began selling off the brick homes. Workers had to then keep the homes up, and they could renovate and modernize. Driving through the village today, most of the homes remain. Many have been flipped and updated. The managers' homes did not all survive. When the mill closed in 1976, the community remained intact. Today, the homes are still owned by some families from the mill days, but most are rented out to college students and young families.

The community would like to be included in the National Register of Historic Places. According to Lydia Simpson, researcher from Middle Tennessee State University Center of Historic Preservation:

Few villages of this type have survived intact to the degree that Riverside has, both structurally and within living memory of community members. The mill shut down in the 1970s and parts of the original manufacturing structures have been continually rented and operated by a variety of

Howard Harwell directs hymn singing at a service of Celanese Methodist Church. Tubize (Celanese), Rome, Georgia, 1970s. Archival images show that the Harwell family lived in the mill village from the 1940s onward. Howard worked in the chemistry laboratory at the rayon mills for many years. *Digital Initiatives, James E. Walker Library, Middle Tennessee State University.*

Left: Tubize Employee's Banquet in the 1940s, Rome, Georgia, 2019. *Rome Area History Museum.*

Below: Tubize security force. Rome, Georgia, 2019. *Rome Area History Museum.*

Opposite, bottom: The Chatillon Corporation broke ground in the late 1920s in north Rome. Portions of the mills remain, and the brick mill homes survived the mill's 1971 closing. *Rome Area History Museum.*

Right: In 1929, Chatillon Corporation, an Italian rayon textile company, built this plant in the Riverside district of north Rome. Tubize (Celanese), Rome, Georgia, 2019. *Author's collection.*

Below: Broken windows in the Celanese plant. Rome, Georgia, 2019. *Author's collection.*

In 1930, Chatillon merged with a Belgian producer, Tubize, and operated as Tubize-Chatillon until after World War II, when British rayon manufacturer Celanese Corporation of America purchased the mill complex and village. Tubize (Celanese), Rome, Georgia, 2019. *Author's collection.*

businesses. Community members hope to use the National Register nomination to draw attention to what they feel is an important part of the cultural landscape in Rome, Georgia and encourage positive, sustainable development and local stewardship.[130]

Having the historic designation means lower taxes and grant monies to preserve the mill homes. Very few of the Celanese homes have been destroyed. The quality construction in the 1920s is the reason for the preservation.[131]

Cherokee/Rome Hosiery Mills, 1902

Neil Power at ten years old. "Turns stockings in Rome Hosiery Mills." Photographer Lewis Hine called him a "shy, pathetic figure." Power said he "hain't been to school much." *Library of Congress.*

A twelve-year-old knitter in the Rome Hosiery Mills. In 1913, she earned four to five dollars per week. April 1913. Lewis Hine, photographer. *Library of Congress.*

Cherokee/Rome Hosiery Mills was the worst offender. Rome Hosiery owned the Cherokee Hosiery Mill, which started production in 1913. Cherokee/ Rome Hosiery Mill ignored the child labor laws. Some of the jobs children were performing included looping and turning. Turners did exactly that—turned the inside-out hosiery to the right-side out. Other children were tasked to pair the socks—they were the smallest, with the least skill. A looper was a skilled job. Children were taught in factory schools not how to read but rather how to loop. Loopers attached the toe to the unfinished sock in a machine.

The mills were noisy and hot, and the windows were sealed shut. Manufacturers needed moist air to avoid the cotton threads from snapping. The lint blowing off the cotton formed a coat over all the children and got into their lungs, creating brown lungs on a smaller scale.

A mill floor is a dangerous place, especially for children. Machines were built for adults, but small hands could reach for bobbins faster than adults. Children were caught in the machines and injured, even maimed. The floors were saturated with machine oils, and children—often barefoot—would slip and fall. Hair got caught in moving pieces. Fingers were pulled off when removing spindles. Hot metal fell from machines, severing limbs. Some children even died.[132]

John N. and H. Roy Berry started something good in Rome. The Rome

Sock turners at Rome Hosiery Mills, with ages nine and ten and upward. The boy in the front in a white shirt is only nine years old. Lewis Hine, photographer. *Library of Congress.*

Hosiery Mill opened in 1902 on the second floor at 434 Broad Street. They moved from the old Chamber of Commerce Building to East Sixth Avenue, the current location of the *Rome News-Tribune.* In 1913, Rome Hosiery bought Cherokee Sock Company on East Seventeenth Street. In 1926, they opened

Noon at Cherokee Hosiery Mills, Rome, Georgia, April 10, 1913. The youngest (eight- and nine-year-olds) are turners and loopers. Lewis Hine, photographer. *Library of Congress.*

Mill Plant No. 2 on Hanks Street in West Rome. By 1930, Rome Hosiery Mill was employing one thousand people and making 1.5 million work socks every year. It was the largest sock manufacturer of men's work socks in the country.

A former employee explained why Rome Hosiery was so successful in the sock business: "When one step was finished it would be at the end of the line for that department, and right at the beginning of the next. There was no wasted time in moving material from department to department."[133] Maybe it worked so well in the beginning because little hands helped the process move along.

SHANNON

Brighton/Burlington Mills, 1925

Brighton Mills was the only cotton mill ever run from New York City. The textile company began in 1879. The first president was Charles M. Pratt.

In 1925, when Brighton was looking for a southern plant location, Shannon, Georgia, was chosen after careful consideration. Easy transportation and ample water were two reasons for settling in Floyd County. In 1926, the Shannon mill started producing tire cord. The official Southern Brighton Mills complex was established in Shannon in 1931.[134]

Shannon did not escape the General Textile Strike. Shannon mill was the only workforce that voted to unionize.[135] The mill unionized and went on strike on Labor Day 1934. Three weeks later, when the strike was not settled, troops came to Shannon. Fourteen people were arrested by the National Guard in Shannon and brought to Atlanta city armory. The arrests were conducted in secret, according to a September 1934 *Atlanta Constitution* account. The military reported that these people threatened the Guard.[136] When the Guard heard the threats, the officers "quietly traced them down and rounded up the men, bringing them to Atlanta. There were no disturbances in connection with the arrests."[137]

The mill village had a different organization compared to most paternalistic mills. The community activities were handled through Associated Brighton Employees Incorporated (ABEI). The ABEI operated the baseball stadium, the park, the swimming pool and the pool hall. It sponsored both the Boy and Girl Scout Troops, the Brighton Textile League Baseball Club, the Brighton Choral Club, the Shannon Orchestra, Saturday night movies at Model School, the Youth Club, the Men's Club, a student loan program and numerous other school and community activities.

The Watters District Council for Historical Preservation is a well-researched and positive website promoting the history of the Shannon area and Brighton Mills. It features several posts from the Brighton newsletter, *Brighton's Warp and Welt Magazine*, published by the ABEI. The December 1947 edition touts the expansion of the Shannon mill village: "Some of the houses will be weather-boarded while others will have an asbestos siding finish. All will be underpinned and finished inside to the satisfaction of the most discriminating."[138]

The president of Brighton Mills sent out a letter to Shannon mill residents about "Victory Gardens" in 1943. This letter explained the situation across America during wartime and revealed his patriotism and concern for his workers and encouraged them to grow vegetables in the mill village. He said, "Under such circumstances it should not be necessary to urge people to take steps themselves to assure their families an abundant supply of fresh vegetables which all of us can produce with very little effort. As a matter of fact, it may be the difference between having a plentiful supply to eat and not having it."[139]

President Morrison wrote editorials in *Warp and Weft* encouraging servicemen during the war years. He wrote letters congratulating employees for buying war bonds; more than 97 percent of Brighton workers pledged to buy war bonds.

In July 1941, the village welcomed Dr. Harry E. Dawson as he opened a clinic for the residents in a newly renovated house. In the company newsletter, the officials of Southern Brighton said they realized that health "is a priceless possession and that once lost is sometimes never regained." *Warp and Weft* continued: "Thus, you see, the clinic is only an additional step in the ceaseless care taken to maintain the enviable health record of our community."[140]

On August 13, 1950, the *New York Times* reported that Burlington Mills had acquired the Shannon Mill and kept the same management. Later, Burlington became Klopman and then Galey and Lord. Slowly, beginning in 2011, the new owners have taken down the final remnants of the mill.

Chapter 8

Gordon County

CALHOUN

Echota Cotton Mills, 1909

The lost town sulks. It has lost its dignity and purpose. As the one remaining stack looks over its loss, it is surrounded by another owner. Sadly, the old smokestack makes up a corner of another company's shipping department in a mismatch of metal buildings and loading docks. The soul is gone from this old textile mill in Calhoun, Georgia.

Like many small North Georgia communities at the turn of the nineteenth century, Gordon wanted in on the growing textile industry. In October 1899, after a massive meeting with all areas of the county represented, they decided to build a cotton mill. Shares to build the mill had to be sold, but big promoters with names like Harbin, McDaniel, Pitts, Chastain and Byrd organized a corporation in 1907. The leaders called it Echota Mills to respect the local area. Gordon County was home to the Eastern Cherokees, whose last capital was New Echota.[141]

Thomas Witherspoon Harbin, the eldest child of Dr. Wylie Harbin, did not become a doctor, and he did not join his father and brothers in building the Harbin Medical Practice. Instead, he built the Echota Cotton Mills in Calhoun. He also became a judge, state senator and religious leader, playing an important part in the development of Gordon County.[142]

The lonely stack of the old Echota Cotton Mills towers over a dilapidated mill village and goes unnoticed by the passing community. A few of the mill homes have been rescued, while nature has reclaimed others. Echota speaks in faint whispers in the shadows of Gordon County, but when it opened in 1909, it was proclaimed to be the "most modern manufacturing plant of its kind," according to a former employee and mill resident. The homes and company store, along with a company school, were constructed in the early 1920s due to the demand for labor. The store was the economic and social center of the Echota Mill Village. The mill, like many southern mill owners at the time, felt that church attendance would enhance production and establish a peaceful community. In 1924, employees organized, and the mill built and maintained Echota Baptist Church.[143]

In the mid-1930s, under the leadership of H.F. Jones, president and treasurer, the mill grew to one hundred employees. The mill did it all. It took raw cotton and converted cotton it into sheeting and coarse yarn at first and later made high-quality sheeting and corduroy. Jones appeared to be an exceptional leader, especially when the mill and his workers were threatened.

Union organizers were clattering all over North Georgia in September 1934. They threatened forceful shutdowns and fights to take over the mills. They were outsiders coming in to force unions on the workers. In a statement issued by H.F. Jones on September 5, 1934, he left the decision to his workers: "I have worked in cotton mills all over the South, and have been

This village home has seen better days, as the vines and grass overcome the old mill house built by the Echota Cotton Mills. *Author's collection.*

managing cotton mill employees for more than 25 years, and I say without reservation that we have the best people and the most satisfactory employees here at Echota that I have ever seen or been associated with."[144]

Jones told the employees that joining the strike was their decision, "but if they decided not to strike, he would use every resource at his disposal to protect them and the plant." Jones told the *Calhoun Times* that the main reason for the nationwide strike was the practice of stretch-outs. Stretch-outs increased the number of machines attended by one employee. Developed to increase productivity beginning in the early 1900s, this was not practiced by Echota Mills. Jones told the newspaper that he did not believe in them. All the employees at Echota voted not to strike.

The fear of the coming union leaders and the "Flying Squadrons" was real. These groups would come into a mill while workers were peaceably doing their job and would harass operatives to join the union and picket. They blocked mill entrances, not allowing workers to come in. They were carrying axe handles and boards with nails, threatening workers and office workers. They were known to turn over cars with mill employees inside. So, Jones closed the mill for fear of bloodshed on September 13, 1934. He closed the mill for one week, but he did not abandon his company.

Jones barricaded the perimeter of the mill with raw cotton bails for protection. His son, Clarence, positioned a Browning machine gun on the roof. A .45-caliber Thompson submachine gun was in the mill office, and overseers were given .38-caliber special revolvers. All the young men were issued picker sticks from the stockroom as they were to patrol the property. It worked.[145]

The union strikers learned of Echota's defensive position and never attempted a coup of this mill. After intimidating the "Flying Squadron" coming their way, they all returned to work on September 17, 1934. In the local paper, an editorial made a statement to the union organizers:

> *What happened in Calhoun may be taken as a fair example of the situation throughout the country. Not a single employee of Echota Mills joined the strike, and yet the mill was forced to close to avoid possible bloodshed. Yet, the total number of employees were counted by the national strike leaders as among those, "out on strike."*[146]

Echota Mills competed internationally until 1985, when cheaper foreign imports stole the textile market from the United States. Before it closed, it was purchased by Mount Vernon Mills in 1970, which tried to keep the mill

Echota Cotton Mills in Calhoun, Georgia. The only thing that remains is this stack, surrounded by a new rug company's trucks and building. *Author's collection.*

alive. According to the *West Georgia Textile Trail*, "[I]n 1979 the mill consumed 7 million pounds of raw cotton with a payroll of $3 million."[147]

After seventy-eight years being sold twice, Echota, though modernized, could not compete with foreign markets.[148] Through all the changes, expansions and retooling, nothing could compete with the foreign markets. The mill slumped into the past, and original walls came down. The solo stack stands awkward in a new world.[149]

Vernon Brookshire, for *Past Times*, remembered the stack as a small child:

> *When I was a small boy, the smokestack that is now the last remaining trace of Echota Cotton Mill was an awesome sight to see. At 110 feet, it was the highest structure in Calhoun....After lightning struck, about 10*

feet were knocked off the top. A man was hired to climb the ladder inside the smokestack and attach a lightning arrestor rod and ground it.

Almost always the smoke flowed southeast by the air current. When coal was first added to the three coal-fired boilers, the smoke billowed black, ominous and angry-like. When the coals became red hot, the smoke turned gray.[150]

The boilers are gone, and the remaining smokestack is stone cold and alone.

CHAPTER 9

Hall County

U nusual weather was not in the forecast for June 1, 1903. That day in Gainesville, Georgia, began with a mix of rain, sunshine and clouds. The only constant was the oppressive temperature and humidity. At noon, heaving inky clouds formed with distant thunder. In an instant, the wind picked up and blew strong from the northeast. A violent whirling motion accompanied clouds rushing in toward this tornado forming. The *Monthly Weather Review* reported in 1903, "The tornado clouds were of the characteristic greenish hue, increasing in their horrible grandeur as they drew nearer. The clouds so closely resembled smoke that man thought it was smoke from an approaching locomotive; the cloud was approaching along the general direction of the Southern Railway."[151] Then the funnel appeared and descended.

Everything was still; for a moment, there was no thunder, no wind and no rain. Then came a deafening roar. The funnel did its work close to the ground. One mile southwest of Gainesville,[152] it hit the Gainesville Cotton Mills at 12:45 p.m. The fourth and fifth floors were smashed in. They had no warning. As the walls fell outward, the roof lifted and was suspended in midair, forming a vacuum over the building. In the *Monthly Weather Review*, it noted, "With a roar and a rush sounding like 'a hundred express trains' the storm came down upon the unsuspecting victims with all its maddening fury. The fury of the gale lasted only a few seconds, when the air became as quiet and still as death for a few moments."[153]

No one had time to prepare. Working on the top floor were 250 children. According to the *Monthly Weather Review*, "Children employed in the spinning room were hurled to the ground and instantly killed. Only two or three bodies were found inside the building, the rest were buried in the debris in front of the building."[154] The fifth floor fell forward in the tornado's path, but the back of the building was intact as the floor slanted at a forty-five-degree angle. The report continued, "Then the rain came down in torrents, accompanied by vivid lightning and wild rolls of thunder. During this time the rescuers worked among the debris. The mill village, however, was intact."

The *Gainesville News* reported in its paper two days later:

> *A most terrific cyclone, about one hundred yards in width, passed over the Southern portion of the city at 1 o'clock Monday afternoon, leaving death and destruction in its path. Houses and trees were swept from the face of the earth as if they were chaff. The cyclone made terrific noise, as if heavy cannonading were in full blast, and as it bore down upon the city, it tore everything in its path. It came from the south west, and no one was aware that it was more than an ordinary thunderstorm until it struck the Gainesville Cotton Mill, which is situated between the Southern, and the Gainesville, Jefferson and Southern Railways. Taking this four-story brick structure, it twisted it as if it were a reed, and in the twinkling of an eye many souls were ushered into eternity. The mill building and store were torn into fragments, and the flying embers were hurled several hundred feet into the air, together with those persons who were in reach of the fierce monster.*[155]

Most of the employees lived in the village of eighty homes. The homes stood high on a hill above the mill and were untouched by the storm. The storm seemed like it would go in the direction of the center of town, but it turned east and cut a three-hundred-yard path toward the mill village of New Holland.

New Holland is where the Pacolet Mills sits. The mill saw little damage, but village homes suffered. More than 1,300 Pacolet employees lived in the 120 company homes, and 70 homes were destroyed. After leaving the village, the storm subsided, leaving ninety-eight people dead and twice that number injured. In 1903 dollars, the property loss amounted to about $1 million.[156] A newspaper account stated, "Some houses were torn into fragments; others were lifted from their foundations and carried intact for blocks, white roofs sailed like leaves in the air and many persons were picked up and carried over the trees and houses for long distances."[157]

Thirty-three years later, it happened again, but this time three tornados met in the center of town and created havoc in Gainesville. W.M. Brice remembered April 6, 1936:

Seeing two inky black clouds converge, making daylight almost as black as night; seeing trees begin to bend and sway, then hearing a mighty roar as of a hundred airplanes, those same trees lose their hold and fly through the air, houses all around you commence to collapse, brick and timber fly, not knowing what moment the hand of death would fall, is a terrifying experience, impossible to describe unless you've felt it.[158]

The storm came after Pacolet Mill at New Holland. Some workers remembered the 1903 tornado, evacuated the top floors and found safety in the mill's northeast end. A worker recounted his experience in the mill that day: "Yes, sir, the clouds looked funny and we heard the roar. Everybody piled down as they saw it coming. It looked like two clouds fighting to get at one another and bumping one another off. We could see things going in the air way over there in Gainesville."[159]

The *Gainesville News* had a firsthand account of the day and the aftermath:

Business houses were closed, and merchants and office men turned to the scene to render aid. That which greeted the eyes of the citizens was horrifying in the extreme. Lying here and there was a man, woman or child with bruised and bleeding body—some even in the last throes of agonizing death—while here and everywhere was strewn timbers, broken wires, limbs of trees, brick, rubbish of every description. It was an awful sight, and many stout hearts broke down and their tears mingled with the wail of the dead and dying.[160]

Gainesville Mills and New Holland (Pacolet No. 4) joined and helped each other in those days. The mills had opened within years of each other and at some point became one company under the leadership of President Victor Montgomery after the death of his father, Captain John H. Montgomery. The mills worked together, according to this Gainesville 1903 account:

At the Pacolet mill, the remains of the dead were gathered up and laid on the first floor of the factory proper. Here they were prepared for burial. There were thirty-three victims in all at New Holland, and President Victor Montgomery estimates the company's loss there at $60,000. About eighty *cottages were swept away, but as there were nearly 100 vacant cottages not destroyed, the homeless were removed to these. The Pacolet mill will start up again tomorrow morning, and those who were thrown out of employment at the Gainesville mill will be transported by the electric line to and from Pacolet at expense of the company.*[161]

The northeast side of the mill was not damaged, but the fourth and fifth floors had collapsed. The mill was heavily damaged. No one was injured. The center of Gainesville was not as lucky. The tornadoes converged in the middle of town and caused the most damage and highest casualties at the Cooper Pants Company.

Before the 1903 storm, Hall County was becoming the textile hub of Georgia. According to *Gainesville Times* columnist and local historian Johnny Vardeman, there have been important days in Hall County history. He cited the railroad coming in the 1870s, colleges coming to town and the formation of Lake Lanier, but "none was more significant than the landing of Pacolet Manufacturing Co. at New Holland in 1900. It was the first sizable industry for the county, though smaller manufacturers were operating. This would be the largest textile mill in Georgia."[162]

A few years later, Pacolet was joined by the Gainesville Cotton Mills. Eventually, it too would be a Pacolet company, and both would bear the brand Milliken.

The latecomer was Johnson & Johnson, bringing a piece of New England to Hall County. In 1927, it named the village Chicopee after a northern town and created a designed mill community. The Chicopee Mill and Village brought attention to Gainesville and Hall County for its professional design. The area continued to be the talk of the state, despite the natural disasters that attacked the area. Its people are resilient overcomers who work together to rebuild. Its character has been known for some time.

In a 1901, a Savannah newspaper praised Gainesville for its "pluck." In the article, "What She Wants, She Gets," Gainesville is portrayed as a woman:

Gainesville wants a new mill and her businessmen put their hands into the pockets and furnished a fair portion of the money to pay for it. They are commended for civic pride and faith in their town. They also show good business judgement. We wish there were more of Gainesville's public spirit and enterprise throughout Georgia. Some of it would do Savannah good.[163]

Hall County has a unique industrial history set in the middle of the textile era in North Georgia. Despite the storms that have devastated the area, the people of the mills were resilient. When the mills came to town, the rural mountain area came alive with innovation and productivity. Each of its three mills has its own story to tell.

NEW HOLLAND

Pacolet No. 4/Milliken, 1900

A special supplement to the *Georgia Cracker* screamed a headline on Saturday, March 17, 1900:

> *A $1,000,000. Mill. Now a Settled Fact that Big Factory Will Be Built Here. 850 Acres of Land Bought at New Holland Springs. Mill Will Run 50,000 Spindles and Consume Annually 430,000 Bales Cotton.—5 Story Building to Be Erected.—the Full Story of The Great Enterprise.*[164]

Gainesville was excited. This was a big deal for Hall County, as this would bring the largest cotton mill to the area. The *Georgia Cracker* was the precursor to the *Gainesville Times* and printed the news on Saturdays from the late 1800s until 1902. The paper claimed that Pacolet Manufacturing Company of Pacolet, South Carolina, would employ 1,400 "operatives" (workers) with a monthly payroll between $15,000 and $20,000. The *Cracker* reported, "The daily output of the mill will be about 125,000 yards of sheeting or enough annually to circle the globe." The paper predicted that the population would increase by 3,000. No mention of how they would house those workers, but it described the mill area:

> *Many changes will necessarily be made in the property and when all the work is done and the buildings are up it will present the appearance of a nice little city. A prettier location for the mill site cannot be found anywhere in the Piedmont region.*[165]

The 1900 announcement said the Pacolet Manufacturing Company products are shipped directly to China. The article continued, "They have long been dealing with the Chinese and as they are very peculiar people it is plainly evident that high grade goods are manufactured." Despite the cultural indifference, Pacolet had an international trade agreement that was beneficial to Gainesville. This was good news for the area. The paper concludes its announcement with, "No one can truly estimate the great good that will result from the coming of this enterprise. There are wonderful things ahead of us and let everybody put their shoulders to the wheel and push Gainesville forward."[166] The *Georgia Cracker* repeated this announcement in the next Saturday's issue on March 24, 1900—Gainesville was poised for success.

The mill bought the property from Kate Holland, the widow of E.W. Holland, who owned the Limestone Springs and renamed them New Holland Springs, as well as ran a health resort. Pacolet bought the 850 acres and built a five-story plant. They built a community as well. The accompanying village had two hundred homes, a recreation facility, a store, a school, a church, athletic fields and business offices. The company employed 1,400 people, but the village would grow to more than 3,000. To put that in perspective, Gainesville's population was only about 5,000. Hall County had a little more than 20,000 in 1901. The Pacolet Mill was a significant addition to the county. Historian Vardemen recorded a former resident, Osee Bennett, remembering her home in the New Holland mill village:

> *Beautiful landscaped streets were laid out, trees and shrubbery were planted, comfortable attractive houses were built with enough room for a flower garden in the front and a vegetable garden in the rear. Prizes were awarded on each street for the prettiest front yard....Each section of the village was provided with a pasture and cow stalls by the company.*[167]

In the 1920s, the mill added a heated indoor swimming pool, bowling and billiards. You could watch movies for fifteen cents at the Village Movie Theater. And the Baptists and Methodists shared the same company church by alternating weeks. The best addition to the mill village was a doctor. Most mill villages in Georgia had free medical care and at least a nurse on call, but New Holland had Dr. Downey.[168]

The early Gainesville newspaper, the *Georgia Cracker*, announced the relocation of Dr. J.H. Downey of Pacolet, South Carolina, to New Holland. He was the mill's physician. He did remarkable work in Gainesville.[169] His inventions and hospital have left a legacy.

Mills were dangerous places because of accidents and the normal wear and tear on the body. The loud environment made it impossible to warn workers of impending danger. Even the mill's owner, Captain Montgomery, had a fatal fall in the dangerous mill. So, Dr. James Henry Downey had the opportunity to help Pacolet's employees recover quickly from bone fractures.

Before Dr. Downey invented and patented the Downey Fracture Table, injured operatives would have to lie flat in a heavy cast in bed. Downey created this table to allow the bone to be set at an angle so the patient could use a wheelchair—increasing their mobility and speeding recovery. His specialty was treating bone fractures. Later, he left the mill and moved his practice to Gainesville in 1904. He built what would become the first fully accredited hospital in Georgia, the Downey Hospital, but not before he tried to save the owner of the Pacolet Mill and served the mill operatives during a shutdown.

Downey, who got his medical degree in 1887, rushed to the side of the dying Captain Montgomery when he fell sixteen to eighteen feet in his mill in 1902. Downey was inspecting the warehouse with a Mr. Stallworth. He was walking in front of Montgomery when he heard a crash and turned around. According to Stallworth, he saw Montgomery "shoot through the air to the floor beneath." He died within hours. His son, Victor, was notified by telegraph, and he allowed operatives to "take a last look at their great chieftain." The mill shut down.[170]

Two years later, Victor Montgomery was installed as the president of both Gainesville mills—Pacolet and the Gainesville Mill. Then the bottom fell out of the cotton market, and Montgomery was forced to close the New Holland Mill for an indefinite amount of time. According to the *Gainesville News* in 1904, the company's reason for shutting down is that the cotton market was wild and uncertain, and it might be dangerous for the mill to continue operations and get its share of cotton. It already had its usual profit in hand, and sometimes caution was the better part of wisdom to let well enough alone.[171]

President V.M. Montgomery made this statement explaining the situation to the *Gainesville News*:

> *Owing to the present conditions, high price cotton and low-price goods, we find that it is not profitable for us to keep our mills here in operation, so we have decided to close down for an indefinite period. But in doing so, we want to do the best that we possibly can for our help, who have had faith enough in our enterprise to bring their families here for the purpose of making a living. As we are desirous that they will still have the same faith in us and remain just where they are, we made them the following proposition:*

We propose to pay one half time (based on the earnings for the past two or three months), to all who remain, giving the house rent free and will furnish the services to our physician, Dr. Downey, with the usual drugs, as furnished by him, free of any cost whatever to the people occupying houses belonging to our company. We will also grant permission to the people, who desire to do so, of securing work elsewhere, provided they remain in their present homes and report to our office once a week. We mean by this where children are sent to work in other places, the heads of the families remaining here can report to the office instead of the children, thereby saving expense they would incur by returning home once a week. We wish to state further, we expect all people, receiving such help from us, to hold themselves in readiness to resume their present work as soon as we find that we can start up and operate the mill without too disastrous results. We beg to say that we make the above statement in good faith and expect to live up to it, and will now say, most positively, that when the mill does resume operation, that it will be done on the same basis as we have been working for the past several months, and that there will be no collections made, on the resuming of work, for the money, rent, and physician services, during the shutdown.[172]

A little more than three months later, the *Gainesville News* announced that the mill had reopened:

Pacolet Mill Number 4, which closed down some time ago on account of the high price of cotton, stared up again yesterday morning on half time. This news caused joy to a large number of operatives who have either been out of employment since the mill closed or have been at work away from their families elsewhere.[173]

The mill was making standard drill for a few months until it was in full operation by early fall. The company stayed true to its commitment and paid the employees half pay, free rent and medical services.[174] The mill was bought by Milliken and renamed Pacolet Milliken Enterprises; it still owns the property where the New Holland Market stands. The community has dissipated, but New Holland is still relevant.

According to former Georgia first lady Sandra Deal, New Holland has always been the hub of Gainesville. People naturally settled there first. One hundred years later, New Holland and the mill village have had a renaissance. As new businesses come in, the old mill village looks down from its hill and ages. Some of the homes have decayed and most are rented, while others are restored to their 1900s appeal.

The New Holland Methodist Church closed due to small numbers in 2013. The Methodist and Baptists shared the same building. Governor Nathan Deal was married in the New Holland Baptist Church, and his wife fondly remembered living in the village. The old church is being converted into affordable apartments and rebranded as the New Holland Studios. The property around the church may contain inexpensive bungalows and an area for old-fashioned tent meetings. The church that served both Baptists and Methodists will now house people in New Holland. The building will retain its character, and the old church bell was relocated to the front of the building.

The mill is still working as Milliken and Company. With just under two hundred employees, it continues to produce textiles. Former villagers might look at the old mill, with the windows sealed with bricks, and remember their dads hanging out whistling at their children. After school, the kids knew to go close to the brick walls as their working fathers called them over. From the upper windows, the men would wrap a nickel in cotton and drop it to their kids for a Coca-Cola or twenty pieces of candy.[175]

Just as leaders in 1900 were excited that Pacolet Manufacturing Company was coming to town, officials in 2014 boasted about a Kroger Market Place and other new business moving in—like New Holland Professional Park. The village homes that were sold to the workers at one time remain on a hill. In 2014, Milliken and Company donated 16.8 acres to Brenau University for athletic fields. The company that came to town in 1900 continues to support and expand Gainesville.[176]

GAINESVILLE

Vesta/Gainesville Cotton Mills/Pacolet No. 6, 1901

The *Georgia Cracker* announced that a new corporation was coming to Gainesville. Vesta Mills from Charleston, South Carolina, was not satisfied with the labor in Charleston. Because New Holland was in the process of completing a mill in the area, it felt that the move made business sense. One of the owners, Captain John H. Montgomery, was associated with the Pacolet Mill at New Holland.

The new company needed money to relocate, so it asked the town to subscribe $100,000 of the $500,000 needed. New Holland was already helping the economy of the town, so the new mill would be an easy sell. The real issue for the move is a sensitive issue today. Here is the exact wording from the local paper explaining the labor problem the mill encountered in South Carolina:

> The Vesta mills have been operated with negro labor, exclusively, and this has proven unsatisfactory. The white labor here has no superior. The Vesta mills company desires, and will amend their charter, to increase the capital stock and put a new plant. The mills are now making money, but not enough to satisfy the directors, and they have decided to go where they can pay larger dividends. This they will, do in Gainesville.[177]

At a January 1901 meeting, the town raised more than enough to bring the mill to town, despite the inclement weather that kept some of the wealthy citizens at home. The mill manufactured a finer grade of goods than the Pacolet Mills at New Holland. Vesta made twenty-two different kinds of yarn. The four-story building would employ more than 500 people and increase the Gainesville population by 1,500. The same construction company from Boston was set to build Vesta Mills.

As the Vesta Mill went up, the citizens were excited. The *Georgia Cracker* on October 19, 1901, recorded the glee:

> There are lively times at the new Gainesville Cotton Mill these days. The last licks on the interior of the building are being struck and in a few days the carpenters will have completed this work entirely.
>
> Upon every floor there are stacks and stacks of machinery, most of which is being unboxed and set up. The framework of the entire eighty cottages is up and three-fourths of them are ready for occupancy. The mill will start up not later than January 1, 1902. The mill cannot run at full capacity for lack of operatives.[178]

The *Philadelphia Ledger* noticed Vesta cotton "moving from Charleston to Gainesville due to negro labor. The report does not speak well for the establishment of cotton mills to the cotton fields about which so much was said two or three years ago; but what will the company do at Gainesville? Will it find white labor there?" The *Georgia Cracker* via the *Atlanta Constitution* answered this question:

Yes, the Vesta mills will find all the white labor it needs there as the mills whenever established in the south. The southern milling interest has always been and always will be founded upon white labor. It is evident that The Ledger *should come down and investigate the situation. There is a world of development going on here, and we would be glad to have the assistance of* The Ledger *in making the acts known to the world.*[179]

After the mill opened in January 1902, it could only run at half capacity due to labor shortages. Cecil Boswell remembered moving from Jackson County to the Gainesville Cotton Mill Village in 1925. The family moved because the crops "all burned up in the field."

The village brought mountain life to the mill city by having a hog killing during Thanksgiving. All the boys joined in and played football with a real "pig skin." They saved the pig bladder, blew it up and let it dry. When they did not have the natural ball, they used scraps of cotton yard from the mill and made balls. Sports were important to the mill villagers.

In 1939, the mill began selling off housing to residents and others outside the mill. The mill village community was slipping away. Pacolet bought the mill in 1943, and instead of being the distinctive Gainesville Mill, it was now part of a franchise and was renamed Pacolet No. 6 to distinguish it from the New Holland Pacolet/Milliken Mills. Eventually, the mill built in 1897 was closed in 1985.

Another old Gainesville business, Adams Transfer and Storage (established in 1903), infused the old mill with several millions of dollars and moved its business in 1993. Bob Adams felt that the building was perfect: "All the columns in that building are wood, except on the left end of the building. That is solid brick wall, 39½ inches of solid brick."

One of the best parts of the building, according to Adams, was the original mill flooring: "There is 4-by-6-inch pine (floor boards), which go on a diagonal, and all of those floors are maple all over the building."[180] The thick-walled building had character but an unsteady foundation. The Adams family had to shore up the building, which had been constructed over water. Adams said, "That building is built on water—we pump water out every day."[181] He was not sure how they built it, but he was told that they just laid trees down across sand and built the mill. The new owners had to shore up the walls with footing that went down 120 feet. The walls were not the only things the Adamses found to be unstable. Stories linger about the building's past.

After a time, the old mill had a new owner. Morris Multimedia Inc. purchased the building in 2017. The Savannah family-owned business has an interest in preserving historical properties and has saved it for a time from destruction. The Morris company saved a historic district in Savannah and built the Trustees' Garden. Charles H. Morris Jr. said, "As a company, we are interested in finding ways to preserve historic landmarks when it makes good business sense to do so, and we hope to do exciting things with the Gainesville Mill eventually." Morris continued, "Our experience with the Trustees' Garden in Savannah has shown us what a valuable community asset these historic structures can be." As of this writing, the Gainesville Mill building stands, and it is not an apparition. It remains a reminder of a lost time. The building continues to have inhabitants—both real and phantom. At some point, the structures might inhabit a new purpose and let life continue.[182]

CHICOPEE

Johnson & Johnson, 1927

Robert Wood Johnson II came to town in 1925 and purchased the beautiful hilly acreage just four miles south of downtown Gainesville. The Johnson & Johnson company needed to expand due to the need for sterile surgical supplies. The mill was to produce gauze, cheesecloth and other medical products. The mill itself was designed by J.E. Sirrine and Company and was built by Fiske-Carter Construction Company, both from Greenville, South Carolina. Johnson & Johnson moved to Georgia because it was close to the cotton supply. Johnson also fell in love with the land. Johnson wanted to build a new kind of mill and village from the ground up.

With the company's culture of cleanliness and sterility, the homes and buildings were built with that in mind. Operatives were expected to carry out this culture of clean. The company designed a mill with a new approach. Instead of a five-story brick building without ventilation, the new mill looked like a college campus on one level, with plenty of ventilation. The company would produce cheesecloth and surgical gauze in a building with "surgical precision." The walls were tiled with enamel and had large windows for light and air. Even the grounds were professionally landscaped to give a welcoming feel to its employees. The company wanted to enrich their lives inside and outside the mill.

Fiske-Carter built the two hundred homes for the mill employees. There were thirty-one layouts the employees could choose from, and the

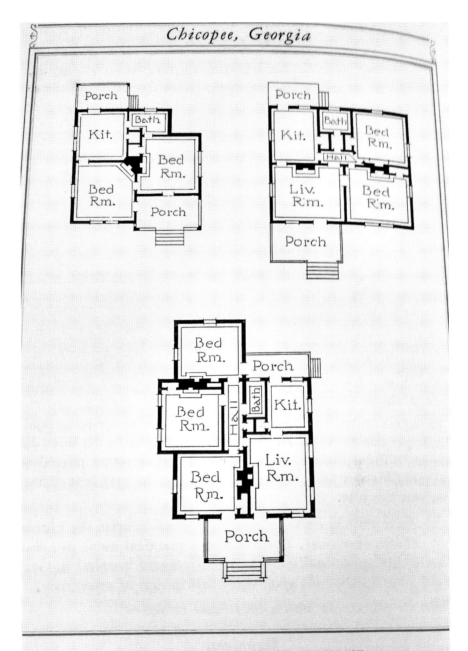

Chicopee house plans. Johnson & Johnson took care to build a modern mill village with modern brick homes. It offered different house plans and rented the homes to workers by the room. The author photographed the manual at the Hargrett Archives at the University of Georgia.

neighborhood was landscaped and planned by E.S. Draper of Charlotte, North Carolina. Johnson wanted Earl S. Draper to design Chicopee Village to match the land and provide work/life separation. He created tree-lined streets and insisted on providing large backyards for gardens and room to play. According to the company's website:

To avoid the cookie-cutter look, families could choose between 31 variations in house designs—all equipped with electricity, modern appliances, indoor plumbing, hot water, and fireplaces. Screened windows ensured that disease-carrying insects couldn't get in, and an expert water filtration and an advanced sewer system contributed to overall public health. To keep the town beautiful and prevent outages during storms, all power and water lines were buried underground. In total, about 250 houses were built in Chicopee.[183]

The paved winding streets were close enough to make it an easy walk to work on the concrete curbs and sidewalks. Most did not have cars. The company wanted to promote good health and exercise by walking to work. The community center sponsored dances and events that encouraged exercise and team sports. Behind the community center, the company put up fields for team sports, tennis courts and a swimming pool. The community had playgrounds and lots of greenspace. Even the store sold fresh fruits and vegetables.[184]

Chicopee was a self-contained community. The store building had a general store, a barbershop, a market and a drugstore. There was a post office, a school, a filling station, a community center and churches. The company was concerned with health, convenience and safety.

Innovation made this mill village unique, down to the streetlights. They were most modern and attractive, with no wires to be blown down or shorted out. Everything was underground. Tunnels under the village, hidden from view, contained the electrical connections, steam pipes and waterworks. The tunnels are still there, and the passageways stretch for thousands of feet.

Johnson & Johnson provided a new life for many of these former farmers, but everything had to be according to the company plan for clean air and water. The water from the company filtration system was pure and clean. Some former residents remembered that everything smelled like fresh cotton sheets coming off the clothesline. Everything had to be in order and progressive—almost staged—even down to the smell in the air.

The mill had fire sprinklers built in and a phone relay system in case of fire. These safety features, common now, were unheard of at the time. The homes had indoor plumbing, hot water, underground electricity and central heating. The employees may have never had these amenities, and for some it was life changing.

The grand social project by Johnson & Johnson may have been intrusive to the workers at home. While the company provided so much, it also required compliance by the operatives in the village. There were rules. Each resident had a copy of the rules. A copy of the village instructional manual is available at the Hargrett Library at the University of Georgia.

The pamphlet reminds the workers that the company "has taken every possible precaution to assure the comfort, safety, health, happiness, and welfare of the workers." The operatives were asked to follow a few rules in their company homes: "keep clean, keep well, keep the peace, and keep strict observances of household, village, and mill regulations." In the booklet, three pages are dedicated to household management, healthcare, village regulations, mill rules and other rules that dictated to the workers how to live in their society. They added regular reminders in the company *Chicopee News*. Included was "The Chicopee Creed." The workers were encouraged to recite and adhere to this creed to make Chicopee a "better and happier place":

THE CHICOPEE CREED
I believe in glad and willing cooperation.
I believe in unquestionable honesty, in the greatest and in the least.
I believe in true comradeship, in enjoying friends because they give me a chance to be my best self.
I believe in loyalty to myself, to my friends, and to my organization.
I believe in being happy, in being glad of life, and glad especially of Chicopee life.
I believe, most, in a life of real service.

Johnson's Social Experiment

Robert Wood Johnson looked at Chicopee in Hall County, Georgia, as an experiment. He wanted the mill and its village to have the latest and the greatest his time and money had to offer. It came at a cost of personal freedom for his employees. That culture of giving back to the community continued until the end, as evidenced by the giving of properties back to the people of Gainesville. His innovations made his mill village unique in rural North Georgia, but his industrial welfare capitalism and the intrusion into the workers' lives eventually caused the same tensions in all the mill villages before and after FDR's failed attempt to fix labor issues—the General Textile Strike of 1934 being one example. Chicopee had its own uprising.

Robert Wood Johnson was an enlightened owner, according to James Lorence in this article in the *Georgia Historical Quarterly*:

> *Johnson believed that a successful business operation required a symbiotic relationship among progressive managers, thoughtful investors, committed workers with a stake in corporate success, and a supportive host community. He rejected a definition of capitalism that solely concentrated wealth in favor of a broader "service capitalism," which earned profit through "service to society" and advanced the "comfort, security, and well-being" of all who depended on progressive businesses.*[185]

Lorence said that Johnson thought the company should provide "good pay, short hours, continuity of employment, and an organized opportunity to present grievances as they arise." The early workers coming from the farms were in awe of Chicopee. They were in desperate need, and this seemed like a panacea. It was new, fresh and modern. The village was a safe place to settle. Johnson wanted to keep reminding the residents how much the company provided.

The company paper, the *Chicopee News*, published from 1928 through 1934, was a method for conveying company policy and creating unity. It had a regular column to teach the residents lessons about community, ambition, sin, honesty and faith in self. The company news constantly reminded the workers that they lived in "the model textile village of the world," where "every available expenditure and preparation [had] been made for [their] comfort and happiness." Chicopee was, it argued, "the place of places in which to live."[186]

The company needed the workers as much as the workers needed the welfare capitalism. Samuel Jones, a retired vice-president of Chicopee Manufacturing Company, admitted that in order to keep an efficient labor force, the management participated in the paternalism that was popular in all the Georgia textile mills at the time. It invested in its workers to keep them happy and at home. The *Chicopee News* made sure that the residents knew the rules of the community. They were required to get regular medical exams, and home inspections were mandatory. Life insurance was offered and encouraged. The company also controlled where they shopped and where they bought their dairy products.[187]

The company navigated through the early Depression years so well that some workers never felt the effects of the economic disaster. Former workers remembered working right through the crisis. The company paper continued to remind them to work hard and be positive—little mention was made of the hardships outside the Chicopee village. But change was coming.

In 1932, Franklin D. Roosevelt was elected, and his plans to help the American worker brought on changes. FDR's National Recovery Administration (NRA) was supposed to free the workers from long hours and little pay, but industry found a way around the rules. Johnson was in full support of the new way because it complemented his philosophy. He was all in—at least at first. However, Johnson eventually grew tired of government entanglements and the textile code authority and decided to have no more "useless discussions with the NRA."[188] Trouble was brewing in paradise, and Chicopee would not come out free and clear of labor wars.

The General Textile Strike of 1934 came and blew past Chicopee at the time, but that was not the end of labor unrest. While there had been efforts to organize the Hall County mills since 1929, the county stayed union free. In 1935, tension between workers and managers at Chicopee was surfacing. Some workers at Chicopee felt that the union might mean autonomy for the workers so used to being under the care of the company. Labor representative John Dajda came to Chicopee and discovered that the company was about to implement the time-study incentive program. Another labor organizer began to hear of the "speed-ups" and "stretch-outs" beginning at Chicopee. The workers at the Johnson & Johnson plant might not have understood what a union was, but they understood the stretch-out.

A form of the time-study system was implemented. Managers did not explain what was happening, and workers feared the new management tool to maximize productivity. Workers were timed and given more work if they took time to rest between starting the machines. The work pace changed because of the pressure of the NRA rules. They would do more work for the same pay. They were expected to keep up the pace. According to worker Clara Mae Cagle, "That's when the war started."[189]

The workers of Chicopee were fed up, and in mid-August 1935, 750 workers walked out in protest. They did not need a union. A small group of workers beat up the "mill clock man," J.H.W. Sneed, the engineer conducting the Chicopee's time-study, and 11 operatives were fired. The union tried to organize during this conflict but was never successful.[190]

President N.L. Smith urged the workers to return to a six-month trial for the time-study incentive and agreed to consider their grievances:

1. *That the point system be abandoned.*
2. *That the eleven employees recently discharged be allowed to return to their jobs.*
3. *That overtime in the mechanical department be paid for in the week in which it occurred.*
4. *That milk and butter be sold at market prices or permission given to approved dairies to distribute in the village.*

By August 28, 1935, Smith had agreed to the last three demands; however, the point system remained unresolved. The parties worked it out by agreeing that the point system would be put on hiatus for two months, and the issue would be revisited at that point. Smith addressed the workers personally and pledged to remain at the plant until all the issues had been resolved. Stretch-outs continued.

The point system came under review, the fired employees returned to work after a cooling-off period and hopefully the milk situation was resolved (although it is not recorded). One problem remained: M.T. Grimes, the authoritarian general manager, was described by the Labor Department as "the source of a great deal of trouble in this mill."[191] The mill reopened in September, but things were not right in the Chicopee family.

Employees were divided and disturbed by fighting in the village late at night and when they walked to the mill. On October 5, 1935, General Manager Grimes suffered a beating. The employees blamed him for the time-study experiment and the point system. This situation was at a continual simmer in the mill. He was jumped outside his home and moved to a remote location.

The company acted quickly, firing and making evictions from the mill. Some workers felt that the company had the right to remove troublemakers. But the mill was targeting not only potential thugs but also those who went on strike. Soon the Chicopee Manufacturing Corporation took a radical step.

On October 20, 1935, the company closed the plant with a tough statement: it did not care to operate under the current conditions. It was referring to the beatings of Sneed and Grimes. While the company offered limited food assistance and credit in the store, it did not have any plans to reopen. Things were not looking good in Chicopee.

The unemployed at Chicopee published an ad in the local paper asking to name the men who beat Grimes. The ad asked, "Shall 1,200 innocent people suffer for the unlawful act of five men?" As a follow-up, former employees joined with community officials at a mass meeting to pledge cooperation with the company "in eliminating all lawlessness and disorder at the plant."[192]

The courts suspended the sentence of the workers who whipped Sneed on November 7, 1935. The management announced the reopening of the mill on January 1, 1936, but would ignore the compromise agreement. However, it replaced M.T. Grimes with J.C. Platt of the Aragon Mills. It created a new management-labor team.

The plant reopened on December 16 with one shift of 250 workers. Soon the workforce was restored to full capacity with 550 operatives. The 200 who participated in the rebellion were not offered jobs. Some felt that the company was cleaning out the troublemakers. The lockout was used to remove the rebels and keep those at peace with Chicopee's paternalism and what it offered on the bargaining table.

In June 1936, Johnson & Johnson gave the employees a 5 percent bonus based on their 1935 wages. Lorence noted in his article about Chicopee, "The company asserted that since 'prosperity largely depends upon the earning power of the people,' the Chicopee Corporation was 'making this contribution to the cause of better times.'"[193]

Johnson supported the Second New Deal, reduced the workweek and increased wages. He moved Chicopee to four thirty-six-hour shifts at a forty-hour wage. He was more progressive than the NRA. Johnson was unpopular when he told crowds that he felt the best way to control unions was to cooperate with the unions. His plant managers did not agree. The textile unions were becoming militant.

These unions tried year after year to infiltrate Chicopee, but the workers did not want them. They were consistently voted out. Just before World War II, they were rejected again just in time for war production. The mill worked 24/7 making surgical gauze for the war effort. After the war, the unions continued to focus on the mill because of Johnson's progressive policies and social capitalism. For those very reasons, the unions never took hold in Chicopee.

Johnson & Johnson celebrated twenty-five years in North Georgia, but times were changing. Like most companies, it began selling off village property and giving away the school to the county. Johnson seemed to regret this decision.[194]

The union was not understood by the people of Chicopee. There may have been a pocket of unionists, but the vast majority rejected it in every vote presented. If they understood, they chose to trust the paternalism to which they had become accustomed. They had developed their own kind of labor-management relations. But when the company stopped being "Daddy" after the 1956 divestiture, Chicopee Mill Village changed. The mill finally closed in 1994.

While businesses have come and gone in the building and the structural integrity of the building has remained, knowledge of the true history and the community's unity has eroded. The first and second generations of villagers remember and have fond memories. Read the company's website with comments from those who lived there and remember the wonderful place they called home.

CHAPTER 10

POLK COUNTY

ARAGON, 1898

It was 1898 when Wolcott and Campbell of New York Mills came to town and created a mill and a town. Aragon appeared on the Polk County maps in 1899, but it was not incorporated until 1914. The State of Georgia took part of Paulding County and named the new county after President Polk on December 20, 1851. The town was named Aragon, a mineral used as a bleaching compound.

Wesley Brumbelow grew up in Aragon and was interviewed in 1988 by another Aragonite, Sam Spence. Spence asked, "How did Aragon get its name?" Brumbelow said, "My grandfather met these two men from New York. They were staying in a hotel in Atlanta named the Aragon....They were sitting one day trying to think of a name for their mill. My grandfather said: 'Why don't you name it after that hotel you like so much?' So, they named it, The Aragon Cotton Mill. That's the way my daddy told it to me."[195]

Aragon was all about the mill. It built houses for the workers. Wesley Brumbelow grew up in Aragon and remembered what the homes were like in the Aragon mill village. When asked if they had electricity and plumbing in the homes, he replied:

> *No! There was no electricity. And the only water they had was an outside hydrant. They had to go outside to get the water. They did not have indoor*

plumbing. They had the houses out in the back alley which were known as outhouses, I guess. And in about 1945, I guess, they built indoor plumbing. They built indoor bathrooms in all the houses.[196]

The mill owners charged rent for these homes and then opened a store that sold everything to the millworkers. According to Brumbelow, "In this store they sold everything. They sold wagons, groceries, dry goods, and everything you could want to buy. Caskets, even."[197] The mill store had a horse and wagon to deliver things to workers' homes. Brumbelow explained, "If somebody died in the community, they delivered the casket to the house. Some of the people would put the body in the casket, then the horse and wagon would take the casket to the cemetery, even in a funeral procession. We didn't have an undertaker."[198]

Millworkers' earnings were a pittance, and they often needed an advance in pay. Brumbelow said, "That's sort of unusual, I thought. It was something the company could do for its employees who couldn't go from pay day to pay day without running out of money."[199] If a family needed money, they paid them on Wednesdays with "loonies," and these metal chips could only be used in the Aragon store. Brumbelow said, "And some people who wanted money would get those 'loonies' on Wednesday and sell them to somebody at a cut rate price, and get the cash. Then those other people would take 'loonies' to the company store to buy their groceries with."[200] On payday, they got paid in cash. Some families did not get much in their pay envelopes because they had to repay their "loonies."

The mills merged with United Merchants and Manufacturers Company of New York. It was 1953, and like most mills at the time, the company started selling the mill homes to renters or other interested parties. That was the beginning of the end; the final straw was the low cost of Japanese imports.

Aragon suffered another strike in 1951. Brumbelow remembered, "It got pretty rough. They didn't want to let anybody in. Of course, the supervisors had to go on in, and I went on in right along. Of course, they would holler at me and say nasty things." He got rocks thrown at him. He carried a shotgun in his car. He was coming home from Rome one night after school, and strikers got in front of his car. He lowered the lights and backed up a little and said, "You'd better get out of my way. I'm going home. I'll run over you if you don't." He put his car in gear and pushed the gas to the floorboard. As he passed, someone yelled "something dirty" at Brumbelow. He stopped his car, backed up and reached for his shotgun and said, "Who said that?…

They all run. They said, 'Nobody.'" The strikers set dynamite under a house and shot into others. They were striking for higher pay.

In mid-August 1970, Aragon mills began the closing process, and the town had to act fast. Aragon was in every sense a mill town. It owned everything and controlled everything. So, in October 1970, the 1914 town charter was validated, and Governor Maddox was sworn in at the city office. A police department was initiated, and the city took charge of water and power. Aragon Mills closed the gates one last time on November 1, 1970. Brumbelow said, "They owned everything. When they sold out, they really sold out.[201]

When folk musician and activist Si Kahn heard of the closing of the mill, he wrote this song:

> *"ARAGON MILLS"*
> *At the east end of town*
> *At the foot of the hill*
> *There's a chimney so tall*
> *Says, Aragon Cotton Mill.*
>
> *But there's no smoke at all*
> *Coming out of the stack*
> *For the mill has closed down*
> *And it's not coming back.*
>
> *I am too old to change*
> *And I am too young to die,*
> *Wonder what will become*
> *Of my old wife and I.*
>
> *There's no children at all,*
> *In those narrow empty streets,*
> *Since the mill has closed down*
> *It's so quiet I can't sleep*
>
> *There's no use anymore*
> *For these cotton mills it seems*
> *But the sound of the loom*
> *still haunts my dreams*

But the only tune I hear
Is the sound of the wind
As it blows through the town
Weave and spin, weave and spin.

Oh, the mill has closed down
It's the only life I know
Wonder what will I do
Where will I go.

But the only tune I hear
Is the sound of the wind
As it blows through the town
Weave and spin, weave and spin.

Si Kahn was an activist and songwriter. He wrote the song just after the mill closed in 1974, listening to a millworker in emotional turmoil.[202]

The mill did continue with new owners and new products until August 6, 2002, when a fire destroyed the remaining complex. A Rome company, Integrated Products, bought the old Aragon Mill in the 1970s to make cotton yarn. The company declared bankruptcy in 1989. David Bridges kept the name when he acquired it, but the doors closed in 1990. Another textile company stepped in.

In October 1990, Diamond Rug and Carpet, a Dalton, Georgia company, operated the plant until 1994. The Aragon property remained silent and empty for four years until brothers Brian and Kirk Spears began producing pillows and pallets there in 1998. Four years later, the buildings went up in smoke.[203]

The Aragon Mill stack remains in stillness and wears its faded name "Aragon" on the brick chimney. Kahn said the mill created the town of Aragon: "This is a way of life that's almost disappeared—part of what built our part of the world, and we're watching it slip away." Kahn called "Aragon Mill" his signature song. The song has been recorded many times by other artists. The melody is haunting, and the words keep a mill village alive. The mills are silent, but many of the former millworkers can still hear the noises: "But the sound of the loom/still haunts my dreams."

CEDARTOWN, 1894

Goodyear, 1925

This mill village was ordered from a catalogue and assembled into a prosperous town. Industrialist Charles Adamson came to town as its first factory owner. He purchased land and set up the Cedartown Cotton Manufacturing Company in 1894. The company grew and took over two other mills in town, the Southern Extension Cotton Mill and Paragon Mills.

After the mill was established, Adamson needed workers, and to attract them, he built them new homes. He ordered thirty-three prefabricated mail-order "home kits" from the Aladdin Company of Bay City, Michigan, and had them assembled in his new mill village.

The Aladdin Company was the innovator of "pre-cut" kit homes. The Aladdin "Redi-Cut Houses" shipped kits of precut, numbered pieces to fill catalogue orders. Two brothers, Otto and William Sovereign, started the business in 1906 and sold more than seventy-five thousand homes until it closed in 1987. They were not alone in this business; they competed with Montgomery Ward and Sears, Roebuck and Company. But Aladdin was the largest mail-order company for these types of home. It cornered the market by building company homes around new mills and plants.

According the company's history, the town of Hopewell, Virginia, was largely developed by the DuPont Company using Aladdin homes. In 1917, Aladdin shipped 252 houses to Birmingham, England, for the Austin Motor Company, which built Austin Village to house workers for munitions, tank and aircraft manufacture during World War I. The small village of Cedartown Cotton Manufacturing Company was started using 33 Aladdin home kits, whose tagline was, "Homes Built in a Day."[204]

Adamson added a mill village playground, a children's nursery and a mission school. He continued to build new homes in Cedartown's west end, but by the mid-1920s, things had begun to change. The new automobile industry required textile products for interiors and for the tires. The tires required a cording to create pneumatic tires. This was an expensive process for most small mill owners, who in turn sold to bigger textile companies. In 1925, Goodyear Tire and Rubber Company purchased the Paragon mills to produce cotton cord and cloth for tires. The early tires required cotton textiles; later tire technology used very little fiber, but in the early twentieth century, cotton was king in the tire business.

A total of 288 homes housed the mill employees. More than 50 percent of the Goodyear employees lived in the mill village. One group was not welcome in the village or the mill. Goodyear Clearwater Mill No. 1 during World War II was in high production mode. Filling in for the white workers who went to war were African Americans. These positions were not given to them before the war. According to the *West Georgia Textile Trail*, "These jobs disappeared after the war and did not return until after Congress passed the Civil Rights Act of 1964."[205] This is a sad fact that is often repeated in the North Georgia mills narrative. The black workers were given the worst jobs, unless there was a shortage of labor. About 15 percent of Polk County is black, slightly less than average for the Piedmont South.

In 1951, both Aragon and Cedartown went out on strike. The Textile Workers Union of America (TWUA) instigated a strike for several months. The *Cedartown Standard* followed the events to the extreme, as in incidents of local businessmen and newspaper editors involved in fights. Polk was a union town; this is not like most of North Georgia mill towns. Industries and the products they make must evolve. Cedartown was tied to the mills, and when it changed, the town changed.

After the introduction of new tire technology in the 1940s, tire fabric was used less, as they developed radial tires using synthetic and steel cords. Very little cotton is used in tire production today. The Goodyear mill closed in 1983. Fire destroyed the closed mill in 1986.

Only a few got rich working in Cedartown's mills. Then, in 1979, the one-hundred-year-old textile plant shut down, leaving the town of 8,500 without six hundred better-paying union jobs.

Although the Goodyear mill is gone, the mill village remains. Homes built by both Charles Adamson and Goodyear are still on the west side of town. The irony is that Adamson was the catalyst for the early prosperity of Cedartown. Due to changes in textiles, he lost his fortune and died a pauper in 1931. He is buried at Greenwood Cemetery in his Cedartown.[206]

Looking back thirty-nine years, and after he sold out to Goodyear, Adamson said in a 1926 *Cedartown Standard* interview, "Cedartown was a small country village on a railroad running from no place to nowhere when I first came here. It is now a thriving town of about 8,000 in population with paved streets and sidewalks, a magnificent school system, and every comfort of a large city." Adamson made a prediction that the Cedartown Mill, and his other contributions "will stand as a monument to his memory." Some may be cynical and point out that the mill is gone and so is the library he built. But it has been more than one hundred years, and he is still tied to his beloved Cedartown. His voice is not silenced, and his legacy lives on.[207]

ROCKMART, 1929

Goodyear, 1929

Rock Mart ("Rock Market") became Rockmart on December 1, 1924. Five years later, Goodyear came to town. In 1929, Goodyear Tire and Rubber Company opened its third textile mill in North Georgia. Unlike the Atco and Cedartown mills, the Rockmart mill was the company's first construction.

Rockmart was named for the vast stores of slate, limestone, iron shale and clay in the ground. Some of the town's buildings, like the Rockmart Slate House, currently a venue made mostly of stacked slate, are a reminder of what lies beneath. Slate from Rockmart has been used around the world in places like London and the Golden Gate Bridge.[208]

When Goodyear built its new mill in Rockmart, it built a mill village for the workers. The 300 homes had different styles and different locations depending on your position in the mill. The brick houses across the street

Goodyear Rockmart third shift. *Georgia Archives, Vanishing Georgia Collection, Plk 206-84.*

from the mill's concrete entrance belonged to the supervisors. Known as "Boss Row," these were the prominent homes in the village. The rest of the 180 homes in the village are behind the brick homes.

The remainder of Goodyear Village had rows of similar small wood-frame homes and no parking spaces. They had to park their cars, if they had one, in special garages blocks away from their homes. The price was right for only two or three dollars per week, and they could lease a lot for raising pigs or raise a garden.

The Goodyear Mill in Rockmart produced an unusual variety of items. It began making cotton tire cord and later switched to rayon. It made heavy clothes for duffel bags, cartridge belts, tents and field packs for the military. It closed in 1949 to retool. In 1950, it reopened after removing all cotton and produced only synthetic fibers—rayon and nylon. In 1953, it produced rubberized fabric and items like life rafts, fuel cells for aircraft and land vehicles, pillow tanks, dunnage bags, small bomb parachutes and oil containers. The product it became famous for was all about fun.

In 1965, a large product from Goodyear in Rockmart made children smile on Thanksgiving Day at the Macy's Parade. Linus the Lionhearted balloon flew over New York, but it was made at the Rockmart Mill. Rockmart made it into the parade for several years. The large rubber parade balloons that were made in Rockmart included the Mickey Mouse balloon in 1971 and Kermit the Frog in 1977. Rockmart workers made ninety-two giant balloons for the Macy's Parade. Due to labor costs, this grand production stopped in 1980.[209]

CHAPTER 11

WALKER COUNTY

LAFAYETTE

LaFayette Cotton Mills, 1903

"Each family is allowed to keep a cow and a pig, and have barns located in a pasture adjacent to the village," boasted a 1920 edition of the *Great Southern Weekly for Textile Workers.* "This pasture is equipped with an automatic drinking trough, is absolutely free, and is for the exclusive use of the people of the LaFayette Cotton Mills." This honest appraisal of the mill village continued: "Our village has comfortable and convenient houses, electric lights, running water in each house, and concrete sidewalks for the entire village." According to this mill newsletter, the insistence on cleanliness and sanitation for the purpose of "good health and happiness" was always on the mind of the company. As with many mills at this time, this may be the story, but it may not be the complete truth.

The theme continued in that same weekly newsletter about cleanliness:

> *The city of LaFayette, being peculiarly and picturesquely located between two mountain ranges, has the advantages of health and climate. However, the company has not accepted the natural advantages as sufficient. The mill building is sanitary and well ventilated, and has a complete steam heating system. Flower beds beautify the grounds, and the entire mill property presents a pleasing and delightful appearance.*[210]

Above: Topper at her machine. Walker County Hosiery Mills, Lafayette, Georgia, April 1913. Lewis Hine, photographer. *Library of Congress.*

Opposite: Workers in Walker County Hosiery Mills, Lafayette, Georgia. Lewis Hine, photographer. *Library of Congress.*

The LaFayette Cotton Mills was opened in 1903 by J.E. Patton. In 1946, Lawrence Fabrics Corporation purchased the mills to make "abrasive jeans." Lawrence Fabrics was sold in 1957 and was finally closed in 2004 by the sock company Sunrise Hosiery.[211]

LaFayette is named for the Marquis de Lafayette, the French aristocrat who was a general in the Continental army during the American Revolution. The name is appropriate, as the county is known as the "Queen of the Highlands." LaFayette and Walker County are situated in a beautiful bouquet of mountains. LaFayette is still a textile town. Shaw Industries Inc. manufactures carpet in Walker County.

ROSSVILLE

Richmond Hosiery Mills, 1898

In 1898, Garrett Andrews moved his Chattanooga knitting mill across the border to Rossville in Walker County. The move was designed to expand his business. In Rossville, Georgia, the enlarged plant took an entire city block. The spinning mill had six thousand spindles, a dye house and departments for knitting, boarding, finishing and shipping. The mill, later renamed Richmond Hosiery Mill, made socks for men and women, and a special section was set aside as "hosiery for the 'misses.'" In 1910, the mill had four hundred men, women and children working. That number had increased to seven hundred by 1922. The mill maintained a mill hospital with a trained charge nurse. They also had a school for "half-time" students. One day, a man came to Rossville and took pictures of the children. Those images live forever, exposing a unique time in American industrial history.

The company rented the mill homes to the workers, but they had to send one worker for every room of the house. Families had to choose a

Young girls working in the Richmond Hosiery Company, Rossville, Georgia, December 1910. Lewis Hine, photographer. *Library of Congress.*

smaller home, not live in the village, or send their young children to the mill. Living was cramped, as every room in the house (except the kitchen) was used for sleeping.

Children had little chance for an education, as the mills ran the schools as an extension of the mill. In 1907 and 1908, twelve- to sixteen-year-old children were removed from school to work in the mill. Supervisors called for them when they needed a hand. For the children, the system was rigged to keep them enslaved to the mill with no education to go elsewhere. The very worst of it was that children could not keep their paychecks. They went to their parents. While most probably considered their pay as a way to support the family, there were some who must have resented it.[212]

CHAPTER 12

WHITFIELD COUNTY

DALTON

Crown Cotton Mills, 1884

Imagine a flyover of Dalton, Georgia, in 1885. The Whitfield-Murray Historical Society provided us an aerial view by republishing an article from the *Chattanooga Times*:

> *Dalton, the county site of Whitfield County, Georgia, is situated among the beautiful hills and valleys of North Georgia, located on a lovely plateau, hemmed in by John's Mountain on the west and extended hills on the north and east; and is the tenth city in the state in population, mercantile and manufacturing interest and second to none as a cotton market.*[213]

Crown Cotton Mill had just been built in 1884, and things were going well. The *Chattanooga Times* article confirmed, "Crown cotton mills, though recently built, are doing an excellent business, already filling orders for exportation."[214] Crown was set up for success.

A group of merchants wanted to bring a textile mill to Dalton. The beginnings are shrouded in mystery, but the Hamilton name was always intertwined with Crown Cotton Mills. John Hamilton had a spring and a brick home, now the oldest in Dalton. John died in 1850, and his widow

Above: Crown Cotton Mills Company Store. Lane and Mary Ann Hamilton (descendants of John Hamilton) repurposed the original mills, office, company store and the Hamilton house. The mills have been converted into loft apartments and places for restaurants and shops. This store was donated to the City of Dalton and awaits its new purpose. *Betsy McArthur, Whitfield-Murray Historical Society. Photo by author.*

Opposite, top: Crown Mills Office, now home to the Whitfield-Murray Historical Society. Notice the company sign and the cubby holes for company mail. *Whitfield-Murray Historical Society.*

Opposite, bottom: The Crown Cotton Mills vault in the old company office was built around the cast-iron safe when more space was needed. *Author's collection.*

continued to manage the homestead. Her two sons left for the Civil War. One son, George Hamilton, later sold Hamilton Spring on his family property to the Crown Cotton Company.[215]

The *Dalton Argus* described the mill as looking like a three-story church with a smokestack.[216] Crown Cotton Mills opened with 75 looms and 3,000 spindles using 20 bales of cotton a day, employing 325 mill operatives. By the turn of the century, an eight-hundred-horsepower compound condensing engine and 700 workers were running 250 looms and 10,000 spindles using 40 bales of cotton daily. Crown made wide and narrow duck cloth, osnaburgs and natural yarns. And the growth continued.[217]

Above: This was the first Crown Cotton Mills company safe. When the company outgrew the safe, it constructed a vault in the mill office. The vault and safe are preserved by the Whitfield-Murray Historical Society in the mill office. *Author's collection.*

Right: Company records that date back to the first years of Crown Cotton Mills in the 1880s remain in the company vault. *Author's collection.*

Company books in the Crown Mills vault contain payroll records from 1888. *Author's collection.*

Crown constructed another mill on Chattanooga Avenue, and by 1916, more than one thousand workers were running the mill. As growth continued, Crown Mill merged with Massachusetts-based West Boylston Manufacturing Company in 1925 to open Boylston Crown Mill in southeast Dalton.

Long before Dalton became the "Carpet Capital," it had one of the first large-scale cotton mills in Northwest Georgia. To entice more workers to come off the farms, Crown built a mill village across from the mill. The company store still stands on Chattanooga Avenue, long boarded up. Across the street was the Hamilton House, where the landowner and mill father lived. Today, it is a venue for the historical society. In the old Crown Cotton Mill Office, the Whitfield-Murray Historical Society archives the records of the old mill in an impressive vault with an ancient safe inside.

The Crown Mill Family

The first president of Crown Cotton Mills. *Whitfield-Murray Historical Society.*

Sibyl Queen, who was a child laborer, remembered when her father was disabled and could no longer work in the mill. George Hamilton gave them a house and came to visit: "If there's anything you need, don't hurt to call." Queen said, "That done something to me about the Hamiltons that I will never get away from."

Queen also remembered mill superintendent Frank Springer as a father figure. He commented in front of a plant visitor to Sibyl, "I have just about raised you in the mill, haven't I?" Queen's self-image grew based on her personal relationships with company leaders. She understood that the company thought of her as "nice, decent people"[218]

Douglas Flamming did extensive research and collected oral histories that gave the villagers a voice. Most early workers thought of the mill as part of their family. Mill village culture was a strange mixture of rural frugality they brought from the farm and a new world of industrialism in which they were immersed. No one should assume that these were "poor pushovers." These farmers came with rich tradition of community. Mill villages were the perfect new home for displaced farmers. To the early mill villagers, Crown was home.

Dalton was isolated between 1926 and 1934, and 71 percent of Crown's job applicants were from Whitfield and the surrounding counties of Murray, Gilmer and Gordon.[219] Crown had planned a mill village, but at first, it only built six homes on Pull Tight Hill and offered boarding rooms. For the first fifteen years, it did not offer nonwage benefits. People still came off the farm for a better life.[220]

Flamming shared the story of Lillie Anne Goforth Hill, who called Crown Cotton Mill "The New Canaan." Lillie Anne moved to Dalton with her family in 1927 and began working at Crown Cotton Mill. Her fiancé, Cletus Hill, was living on his family farm in Cleveland, Tennessee. Cletus wanted Lillie to move to the farm after they married. She said, "No way, I've come to Canaan land."

Lillie Anne went to plant superintendent Frank Springer to ask for job for Cletus. This was bold. Frank Springer was not known for offering up jobs so easily. He must have thought a great deal of Lillie. He not only promised a job to her fiancé (if he got to Dalton for work at 6:30 a.m. the next morning) but also allowed her relative to get off work to drive her to Cleveland.[221]

When they got to Cleveland in the middle of the night, Cletus's father was disappointed. He needed him on the farm. But like so many young people at this time, they wanted off the farm. After an arduous trip that involved many tire changes, Cletus made it to work by 6:30 a.m. Lillie and Cletus spent their lives together "with" the Crown Cotton Mill.[222] For Lillie Anne, her family was complete—Cletus and Crown Mills Village.

Many felt that mill life was better than farm life. Sarah Bunch and Anna Nell Gareen were desperate. "We just wanted off the farm." They had relatives at the mill, so in 1927 the entire family moved from Walker County in an "old 22 T-Model."[223]

Some families still worked their farms and sent the younger children to work in the mill. At Redwine's Cove, a rural community south of Dalton, the Gazaway family sent several children to Crown, while the parents and older sons worked the farm. The children lived with cousins in the village and only came home on Saturday afternoons after work.[224]

Between the wars, most people who joined the Crown family were literally family. Workers married one another and perpetuated the family feeling.

An early image of Crown Mills and its employees. Douglas Flamming noted in his profile of Crown Cotton Mills, "Most of the first mill families hailed from north Georgia and boasted substantial numbers of children." By the 1890s, three or more members of each household were working in the mills. *Whitfield-Murray Historical Society.*

To continue familiarity, the village included farm elements such as gardens, cows and hogs. One resident said, "The way that they operated when I was little on Jones Street, I don't think was much different from being on a farm." The village planned for this. It started small but grew with the mill.[225]

The Pull Tight six soon became seventy when Crown expanded in the 1890s. As the mill grew, so did the village. The village grew to 350 homes, rented for one dollar per room for many years. Each home stood six feet apart on a quarter acre. The company planned for family vegetable gardens. This was important to the transient farmers, and it supplied the family with food supplements. This helped them preserve the farm environment. When it did build, it built cheap, with no running water, electricity or bathrooms.[226]

The workers hated not having water close by, so water was put in the homes in 1888. The clapboard homes had tin roofs and brick pillars for foundations. Coal-burning fireplaces heated these single dwellings, but they had to share a privy with four households in outdoor "eight-holers." The homes were not fancy, but it was all very familiar.[227] When the mill villages were built, residents felt that these nonwage benefits led to the paternalism system.

Crown provided the homes for one dollar per room per week. In the 1920s, it added electricity—better than most had in the hills where they had migrated from. The company installed one hanging lightbulb per room, but with no outlets. The company emptied the outhouses behind the homes. Some felt that they were living in high cotton compared to life on the farm. The waiting list for a mill village house was long.

The villagers stayed on the wait list to move around for better homes and more preferred streets. They formed groups on the streets and socialized after hours. They had a distinct time when they did not have to work—from Saturday afternoon until Monday morning. Women worked all the time. This was not very different from farm work, but it was very different for the men. For the first time, they had time off work.

Social Status in the Crown Mill Village

Dalton has always seemed to have a silent social order that was hard to understand and harder to break. The "uptown" middle class of Dalton did not want to associate with the "lint heads" and called them white trash. The millworkers resented that and responded that Crown does not hire trash. Uptown boys and girls were not supposed to mix, and they were never invited to each other's homes. The mill village residents gave their white trash label to the residents of "Happy Top," where black and white residents mixed. While the wealthier town people excluded the mill village people in social events, Crown Mill residents created their own social order within the confines of the mill village.

A carryover from farm life was how you kept your yard. If you had a messy yard, you were trash. The mill jumped in on this and started a contest for the best yard. For several years, the families competed. Whether it was from paternalistic favoritism or just superior yard skills, one family won year after year until the conflict caused the mill to stop sponsoring the contest.

One group of people was not even considered in the social order of mill life. From the day it opened in 1885 until it shut down in 1969, "Crown never employed a black person, partly because of the racial biases of the managers and partly because, had a black person been hired, the while mill hands probably would have revolted, as they had in Rome and Atlanta during earlier decades."[228] The local black residents wanted nothing to do with the white millworkers.

African Americans avoided Crown Mill and other villages. Lynching was a sport by poor whites during the time. The attitude was remembered by one village resident when asked if a black family could move into the village. She said that the idea was "literally unspeakable."[229]

Another group that isolated themselves from mill villagers were Christian workers. In 1908, the Pentecostal Holiness movement invaded the mostly Baptist and Methodist region. The Church of God had a stronghold, and it was supportive of the mill village rules and judgmental of those who did not value its brand of Christianity, including its mill village neighbors.[230]

The mill had rules against drinking and gambling. The Pentecostals supported these rules. The mill encouraged church attendance and helped organize Crown View Baptist Church. Tent revivals were regular events. After one powerful revival, it spread to the mill floor. Workers were jumping up and down and shouting and disrupting work around the looms. Finally, Superintendent Frank Springer had to shut the mill down until the religious fever subsided. Crown Cotton Mills accommodated the workers by providing company events for the precious off hours.

The mill provided athletic teams for girls and boys. The company built a tennis court at the request of the young millworkers. It built a huge stadium for the textile baseball league to compete with regional teams. Like most mills, good players were recruited and given jobs in the mill. Superintendent Springer did not approve of the practice, but for the good of mill morale, he relented.

The lives of the mill operatives were loosely woven into the purposes of the mills. Paternalism provided a home, a church, a store, a baseball team and a set of rules. When economic times began to change, this weave began to fail, and the children started to rebel. Roosevelt's New Deal instituted the National Recovery Act. Someone bigger than the "Mill Daddy" sent down laws to improve lives of the workers. Change is never easy, and the relationship was changing.

Things had gotten hostile between management and workers by this time. Before, the former farmers respected the paternalistic system that they learned about in rural community life. Things were getting hostile. Favoritism was evident. A man was fired by Superintendent Springer on a tip from one of his favorites that someone had a chicken in his yard. The offender was fired but totally innocent. The rebellion grew.

Workers were not allowed to bring cokes or food to the mill floor. Some of the male workers then went to the store and bought Coca-Colas. At the mill, they tied the bottles to a rope lowered from the third floor, and they were pulled up for the thirsty workers.

One day, Superintendent Frank Springer went through the mill to declare that dipping snuff was prohibited. In response, a disgruntled worker leaned out the window and spat out a mouthful on Springer's head. Another rule—that women were required to wear cotton hose in the mill—was mocked. One female employee refused to wear them into work due to the heat. But when Springer made his rounds, somehow that woman got those hose on before he saw.[231]

Life was getting harder, and the pressure from the mills was not helping. Financially, the workers lived from paycheck to paycheck, and creditors often took from the paycheck. Millworkers were only paid once every two weeks, so small local groceries set up credit accounts for them. They could never get ahead.

Families knew what it was like to "make do"—they had brought it with them from the farm. Children working the mill was natural to farmers, whose children were often forced to help the family survive on the farm.[232] Some families took advantage of the new growing home industry of bedspread work to bring in extra income. The villagers helped one another.

The Crown Mill Failure

Amid the Great Depression, paternalism fell apart. In his book *Creating the Modern South, Mill Hands and Managers in Dalton, Georgia 1884–1984*, Douglas

Flamming said, "Cotton-mill paternalism ultimately rested on a false promise. To those families who remained loyal, the corporation offered an implicit guarantee that steady employment would be available."[233] With New Deal solutions and the downturn in production, Crown was ripe for the union organization. The family was breaking apart.

Management instituted stretch-outs and shared time. Families were coming home with less money. Paternalism often breeds favoritism, and preferred employees were given more hours and better positions. Crown was able to stay open longer than most because of the Ford Motor Company orders for tire linings and car interiors. Workers began to organize early in the 1930s and were pitted not only against management but also against one another.

The organization process took place in secret. In 1933, Local No. 1893 of the United Textile Workers of America (UTW) formed at Crown. Union organizer Tom Crow had workers coming to his Trammel Street home to sign union pledge cards in the middle of the night. Crown had created a web of information-gathering and employed spies like other mills to know what labor was doing. It would fire anyone talking about unions. Somehow, this effort went undetected. When Crow asked to meet with the Hamiltons and Will Moore, they were taken off-guard.

On October 11, 1933, when Tom Crow and other union workers met with the management, they were working as they always had in the rural South. They were uniting for a good cause as a community. The management had answers for their complaints. About the "speed-ups" and "stretch-outs," they were a result of faster machines. As for the unfair firings blamed on favoritism, the management said they would investigate. Nothing was settled.[234]

The 1933 National Industrial Recovery Act (NIRA) tried to send workers back to work. It worked out production codes for troubled industry. What the people working in textile mills heard Roosevelt say was to strike. He did not say that, and FDR was not listening. So, on September 1, 1934, the textile workers across the country went on strike.[235]

In Dalton, Saturday, September 1, 1933, was a half-workday. Mill hands met downtown for a mass meeting. On Monday, Labor Day, the largest Labor Day Rally ever held in Dalton included 1,500 union workers representing every trade organization in Dalton. The parade route included a walk through Dalton's main business district and along the tree-lined Thornton Avenue, where the wealthy merchants and industrialists lived.

The Crown management showed its distance from their workers by saying, "We know no more about the strike than what we read in the papers.

And will be closed until further notice."[236] The Hamiltons went fishing. It was good for business. They had a full inventory that was not selling. This would lower production costs. Paternalism was fading away.

The workers remember the 1934 general strike as a picnic. Sarah Bunch said they had a ball. Picketing was a symbolic gesture, as 450 men and women in groups of 20 manned the picket lines for twenty-four hours in three shifts. While other mills had wars breaking out and machine guns mounted to mill roofs, Crown had community events outside the mill gates.[237]

Finally, Roosevelt called off the National Strike on September 21, and Crown returned to work without retribution. This was not a huge shift, but rather a warning of what was coming. Management accepted Local No. 1893, not as a union but as a committee and allowed it to bring grievances to the company. Leaders Hamilton and Will Moore handled the union with restraint.[238]

Even with management's acceptance of the union in the mill, a much harder test would come in five years. The strike in 1939 would pit worker against management as well as worker against worker. The four-month strike was only broken when the workers broke the line at Boylston and then at Mill No. 2 at Crown. Things got heated between workers, and some rifts were never healed.[239]

Will Moore died shortly after the 1934 strike, as did Superintendent Frank Springer. Labor costs grew, and the union was blamed. Local No. 185 saw this as aggression by new leader "Little George" Hamilton. The millworkers had yet to see raises after a contract was signed in 1938. Tensions rose as the company increased workloads and proposed a 10 to 20 percent wage cut.[240]

On May 30, 1939, hundreds of pickets at Crown and Crown Boylston Mill blocked entrances, and in some cases, small fights broke out. Human walls would not let nonunion workers in, not until July, when a judge ordered the also striking workers at American Thread mill across town to allow nonunion workers in. Then Crown nonunion workers broke the picket line. This strike left paternalism in pieces in Crown Mill Village. Something had changed, and then World War II intervened.

The War Effort

Often when remembering the war effort of World War II, we think in terms of glowing camaraderie in the trenches and at home. While this is true, the war changed Crown Mills and its people. By the end of the 1930s, child labor laws had taken the children out of the mill and into school. The workweek was limited to eight-hour days and overtime pay. People could get unemployment and Social Security benefits. Unions were sanctioned by the government and were required to stand down during the war. America's welfare state encroached on welfare capitalism and putting an end to paternalism in the mill village.[241]

The war had a powerful effect on the Depression and mill families. Women began working in the mills, and the mills began to provide childcare with community support. The family economy got better with more work. Since the government was footing the bill, workers were paid weekly instead of biweekly. Crown Mills made a tremendous profit from the war effort. But there was a cost. Crown workers were required to produce at a higher rate for the war effort. The tent duck material they were forced to produce was a difficult product. With increased production and an inexperienced labor force, accidents increased.[242]

The duck needed by the government was considered critical throughout the war. George Hamilton Jr was concerned: "We want to and of course will cooperate with this program to the fullest of our ability. We only wish though that it was on some construction which is not so difficult to make and which we had not done so well within the past. We do not want to promise a delivery on which we might fall down."[243]

Mill people were no longer isolated, but rather were part of the larger world. The southern workers were given a chance to have their voice heard. There was a different conversation in the news about hardworking people and the war effort. Before, the Dalton paper ignored the workers; now they were front-page news as they toiled to meet war quotas. The social order had changed, but that would not last.

When the war ended, some men came back to work. They were guaranteed jobs, but things had changed and some did not want to work in the mill. David Hamilton, the new president of Crown, said that it was like the old song: "How you gonna keep 'em down on the farm after they've seen Paris?"[244] They wanted more for their children. They wanted them to go to school and go out into the world. People were leaving the mill village for better jobs and education and because they had a car to commute to work. As the children went to high school in the 1940s and 1950s, they never returned to the mill. Flamming said it was a "collective walk out of the mills."[245]

Crown Mills diversified and closed the mill in 1969, mostly for economic reasons. Crown was losing money, and labor fights only made the problem worse. Some think that the union shut down the textile mills—that was only

Helen working the spindles at Crown Mills. *Whitfield-Murray Historical Society.*

part of the problem, although it was still a problem. The union had fallen out of touch with its members, and four months after Crown closed, an insistent letter came from the offices of the TWUA asking for information on the mill. Across the letter an employee had written, "This plant has discontinued operations at this location. There are no employees working in the plant at this time."[246]

DALTON

American Thread Company, 1920

July 12, 1944, was a special day at the American Thread Company on the south side of Dalton. The U.S. War Department was coming to town to present the mill with the sought-after Army-Navy "E" Award to reward production. The award was a pennant for the plant and emblems for all plant employees.

With all the dignitaries in attendance and the news reels recording, the most significant event occurred when Irene Bailey took the podium and spoke for the American Thread millworkers and the union. The entire speech was printed on the front page of the *Dalton Daily Citizen News* the following day.

Bailey pledged that workers were making their best efforts to crush the Nazis and Fascists by working hard to supply the effort. Her themes of patriotism, hard work, union solidarity and freedom were articulated with intelligence:

> *Ours is the only country in the world today, where working people enjoy the full and unrestricted rights of collective bargaining. It is through that process that we have worked out our problems with our company and as a result, a friendly and harmonious relationship exists today. The road to winning this honor has not been easy—you, my fellow workers, have toiled long and tirelessly, day in and day out—you have stuck to your job and you have done a good job.*

While giving a nod to management, she continued. "But it is you, my fellow workers, who deserve the major part of this great honor. We are proud of our country, proud of our company, and proud of our Union."[247] Things had changed for the millworkers that day. They finally got the respect of the community that they deserved.

In 1937, the five hundred workers at American Thread walked out for a long period in protest over the stretch-out system it had instituted. Two years later, in solidarity with Crown, five hundred American Thread employees walked out in protest.[248]

Anti-unionists went to court to prevent pickets from blocking the American Thread Mill entrance. With a highly charged audience, in five days, Superior Court judge John C. Mitch finally granted an injunction on Saturday, July 7, 1939. He limited the pickets at Thread Mill to only a few. This allowed one-quarter of the mill hands to go back to work on Monday. This began a domino effect for the other striking mills. This was a serious hit on American Thread Mill Local No. 124.[249]

The company-owned homes were sold to employees in May 1950. The announcement sounded like an opportunity of a lifetime: "Employees for the local plant of American Thread Company are given an opportunity that every American wants: home ownership." All 120 homes were offered to workers living in them first, with easy terms and small down payments. A later *Citizen* newspaper article showed the employees adding rooms, garages, driveways, porches and a new coat of paint. The article was titled, "Home Ownership."

Textile labor newsletters offered their opinion: "Problem of the Mill Village: Employers Trying to Unload Worn-Out Houses on the Workers." They claimed that mill owners were forcing employees to buy "on the good old installment plan" the shacks that they had been renting for years. The message, noted the union paper, was that "paternalism no longer pays."[250]

American Thread Company closed in 1965, citing union struggles. American Thread employees were strong and stood up not just for themselves but also for other workers in other mills. Their legacy made working in carpet mills in the future easier for the laborers.

THE FINAL WHISTLE

The mill machines slowed in a disorganized symphony with an adagio ending. The textile era was over. The mill village cottages were sold to renters and landlords in the beginning in the 1940s and continued until no mill-owned villages exist. This unique time had ended. Most of the mills closed and remained silent, while others came back to life as repurposed places.

Buildings like in Shannon were bought and sold and then bulldozed. Others were renovated into chic industrial lofts with open spaces and pieces of the past embedded in the walls and environment. Aragon and New Echota have cold stone stacks standing as an anachronism of this lost era. The final whistle has blown, and time has moved on.

NOTES

Chapter 1

1. Trimble, "Soil Erosion."
2. Rawlings, "Myth of the Boll Weevil."
3. Ibid.
4. Flamming, *Creating the Modern South*, 29.
5. Georgia State University Library Research Guides, "Southern Labor Archives."
6. Ibid.
7. *Uprising of '34*, DVD.
8. Ibid.
9. Dufresne, "Georgia."
10. Johnson & Johnson—Our Story, "Building Chicopee Mill and Village."
11. *Uprising of '34*, DVD.
12. Kidd, "Remembering Shannon Mill Work," personal interview.
13. *Uprising of '34*, DVD.
14. National Child Labor Committee, *Child Labor in Georgia*.
15. National Child Labor Committee Collection, "Arrangement and Access."
16. Dufresne, "Georgia."
17. Ibid.
18. *Gainesville Times*, "Gainesville Mill."

19. Gibbons, personal interview.
20. Shores, "Working to Play, Playing to Work."
21. Gibbons, personal interview.
22. Bostwick, "Take Me Out to the Ballgame."
23. Sloop, "Rudy York."
24. Ibid.
25. Ibid.
26. Bostwick, "Take Me Out to the Ballgame."
27. *Atlanta Constitution*, "14 Are Arrested at Shannon Mill," 3.
28. Ibid.
29. Ibid.

Chapter 2

30. Etowah Valley Historical Society, "Atco School."
31. Bowen, "Education Is a Gut Issue for Harris," 25.
32. Russell, *Lost Towns of North Georgia*.
33. Bryson interview.
34. *Wing Foot Clan*, "Billion-a-Month for Victory," 1.
35. *Wing Foot Clan*, "Another Promotion of Interest," 1.
36. *Wing Foot Clan*, "Emma Gillespie Is Atco's Largest Girl."
37. *Carroll Free Press*, "Georgia Weekly Press Association Party."
38. Russell, *Lost Towns of North Georgia*.

Chapter 3

39. *Past Times News Publishing Company*, "Chattooga County," 37.
40. Ibid., 39.
41. *West Georgia Textile Heritage Trail*, "Berryton."
42. Ibid.
43. Creative Home, "EverStrand Carpet."
44. *Atlanta Constitution*, "Summerville Cotton Mills," 6.
45. *West Georgia Textile Heritage Trail*, "Summerville."
46. *Atlanta Constitution*, "Summerville Cotton Mills," 6.
47. Ibid.
48. Ibid.

49. Ibid.; Original Poems and Family History Blog, "First Baptist Church Summerville Georgia."
50. *West Georgia Textile Heritage Trail*, "Summerville."
51. Hayes, "Night General Sherman Stayed in Trion."
52. Ibid. Note: Some accounts say that General Sherman stayed at the old Ragland House, which was located across the street from the cotton mill. Obviously, the Allgoods suggested that the general stayed with them for at least part of the evening
53. Cooper, letter to family member.
54. Ibid.
55. Mount Vernon Mills Inc., "Denim."
56. Cain, "Cotton Mills of the South."
57. Mount Vernon Mills Inc., "Denim."
58. *Atlanta Constitution*, "AllGood Shot Dead."
59. Ibid.
60. Ibid.
61. Ibid.
62. Ibid.
63. Mount Vernon Mills Inc., "Denim."
64. Ibid.
65. Cain, "Cotton Mills of the South."
66. Baker, *Chattooga*.
67. *Brief History of Trion*, 29.
68. Ibid., 19.
69. Ibid., 90.
70. Ibid., 29.
71. McCollum, *Chattooga County*, 46.
72. Mount Vernon Mills Inc., "Denim."
73. McCollum, *Chattooga County*, 46.
74. Mount Vernon Mills Inc., "Denim."
75. Ibid. Note: Greige is an unfinished woven or knitted fabric that hasn't been bleached or dyed. It can be used for upholstery, window treatments, clothes and other textiles.
76. Mount Vernon Mills Inc., "Denim"; *West Georgia Textile Heritage Trail*, "Trion"; Cooksey, "Chattooga County."
77. Hayes, personal interview.
78. *Brief History of Trion*, 17–19.

Chapter 4

79. McCanless, *Story of a Man, a Town and a Mill*, 2.
80. Jones, "Cotton Mill Situation."
81. Rock Barn Cherokee Historical Society, "Canton Cotton Mill #2."
82. Lee, "Story of Asaph Perry."
83. Ibid.
84. McCanless, *Story of a Man, a Town and a Mill*.
85. Rock Barn Cherokee Historical Society, "Canton Cotton Mill #2."
86. Cauley, "Our Town," xx.
87. Mill on Etowah, "Canton, Georgia."
88. Ibid.

Chapter 5

89. Lat34North, "Clarkdale Historic District c. 1931."
90. City of Austell, Georgia, "Threadmill Complex History."
91. *Marietta Daily Journal*, "What's the Difference Between Acworth and Clarkdale Thread Mills?"
92. Ibid.
93. *Marietta Daily Journal*, "Former Threadmill Workers Spin Yarns."
94. City of Austell, Georgia, "Threadmill Complex History."
95. Cunningham, "Cobb County's Old Clarkdale Park."
96. Petite, *Women Will Howl*, 147
97. Rylands, "Long Walk Home."
98. Petite, *Women Will Howl*, 147.
99. Roswell Women, "Roswell Civil War."

Chapter 6

100. Proctor, "Douglas County."
101. *West Georgia Textile Heritage Trail*, "Douglasville."
102. Martin, "Mill Women and Children of Roswell."
103. Petite, *Women Will Howl*, 154–55.

Chapter 7

104. Longworth, "Behind the Strike."
105. Daly, *Testimony of H.P. Meikleham.*
106. Wright, "Meikleham," presentation.
107. Wilder, "Pepperell Students Preserving Stories of Mill Town."
108. Russell, *Lost Towns of North Georgia.*
109. Ibid.
110. Hicks, *Family History of Joseph Wilson Hicks.*
111. Ibid.
112. Ibid.
113. Ibid.
114. Ibid.
115. Ibid.
116. Ibid.
117. Popham, interview.
118. Jackson, *Lindale.*
119. Russell, *Lost Towns of North Georgia.*
120. Ibid.
121. Ibid.
122. Lindale Mill Filming, "The Mill."
123. Gable, "Anchor Duck Monument."
124. Ragland, "Guest Column: Rome Hosiery Mill Once Led Nation."
125. Mosely, "Anchor Duck Mills."
126. *Past Times News Publishing Company,* "Anchor Duck," 24.
127. Ibid., 26.
128. Ibid.
129. Ragland, "Guest Column: History of Rome's Anchor Duck."
130. Simpson, "In Progress: Celanese Digital Collection."
131. Walker, "Shannon Mill."
132. Dufresne, "Georgia."
133. Ragland, "Guest Column: Rome Hosiery Mill Once Led Nation."
134. Watters District Council for Historic Preservation, "Watters District Council."
135. Brattain, "Labor's Best Friend," 49.
136. *Atlanta Constitution,* "14 Are Arrested at Shannon Mill," 3.
137. Ibid.
138. Watters District Council for Historic Preservation, "Watters."
139. Ibid., "Watters District Council."
140. Ibid.

Chapter 8

141. Brookshire, "Echota Most Modern of Its Kind," 37.
142. Ibid.
143. Ibid.
144. Ibid.
145. Ibid.
146. *Calhoun Times*, September 20, 1934.
147. Brookshire, "Echota Most Modern of Its Kind," 38.
148. Ibid.
149. *West Georgia Textile Heritage Trail*, "Calhoun."
150. Brookshire, "Echota Most Modern of Its Kind," 38.

Chapter 9

151. Marbury, *U.S. Weather Bureau Monthly Weather Review*, 268.
152. Ibid., 206.
153. Ibid., 268.
154. Ibid., 269.
155. *Gainesville News*, June 3, 1903.
156. Marbury, *U.S. Weather Bureau Monthly Weather Review*, 269.
157. GenDisasters, "Gainesville, GA Tornado, Jun 1903"; Marbury, *U.S. Weather Bureau Monthly Weather Review*.
158. *Atlanta Journal*, "Man Who 'Broke' News of Tragedy," 15.
159. *Atlanta Constitution*, "Scenes of Unforgettable Horror," 16.
160. *Gainesville News*, June 3, 1903.
161. Ibid.
162. Vardeman, "MilliKids Kept Plenty Busy."
163. *Georgia Cracker*, "What She Wants, She Gets."
164. Georgia Historic Newspapers.
165. Ibid.
166. Ibid.
167. Ibid.
168. Vardeman, "MilliKids Kept Plenty Busy."
169. *Georgia Cracker*, "Dr. J.H. Downey of Pacolet."
170. *Gainesville News*, November 5, 1902.
171. *Gainesville News*, February 3, 1904.
172. Ibid.

173. *Gainesville News*, May 18, 1904.
174. Ibid.
175. King, "New Holland."
176. Gill, "New Holland a New Village Rising."
177. *Georgia Cracker*, "Gainesville Vesta Mills."
178. *Georgia Cracker*, October 19, 1901.
179. *Georgia Cracker*, "Come Down and See."
180. Bates, "Weaving Tales: Once the Home of a Cotton Mill."
181. Ibid.
182. *Gainesville Times*, "Times Parent Company Buys Historic Gainesville Mill."
183. Johnson & Johnson—Our Story, "Building Chicopee Mill and Village."
184. Kilmer House—Johnson & Johnson.
185. Lorence, "Workers of Chicopee."
186. Ibid.
187. Ibid.
188. Ibid.
189. Ibid.
190. Ibid.
191. Ibid.
192. Ibid.
193. Ibid.
194. Ibid.

Chapter 10

195. Brumbelow, "Mill Workers Oral Histories (MC 109)."
196. Ibid.
197. Ibid.
198. Ibid.
199. Ibid.
200. Ibid.
201. Ibid.
202. Andy Irvine Lyrics, "Aragon Mills."
203. *West Georgia Textile Heritage Trail*, "Aragon."
204. Aladdin Company of Bay City.
205. *West Georgia Textile Heritage Trail*, "Cedartown."
206. Ibid.

207. Gray, "Cedartown Cotton Company."
208. Rockmart History Museum, "Historic Rockmart"; *Northwest Georgia News*, "Polk's Past Mills Provide Tourism Opportunities."
209. *West Georgia Textile Heritage Trail*, "Rockmart."

Chapter 11

210. *Mill News*, "Lafayette Cotton Mills," 82.
211. *West Georgia Textile Heritage Trail*, "Lafayette."
212. Hall et al., *Like a Family*, 127–29, 162.

Chapter 12

213. Gudger, "Dalton, the Chief City," 51.
214. Ibid.
215. Flamming, *Creating the Modern South*, 38.
216. Ibid.
217. New Georgia Encyclopedia, "Crown Cotton Mill."
218. Flamming, *Creating the Modern South*, 170.
219. Ibid., 190.
220. Ibid., 160.
221. Ibid., 179.
222. Ibid., 182.
223. Ibid., 189.
224. Ibid., 190.
225. Ibid.
226. Ibid., 161.
227. Ibid.
228. Ibid., 199.
229. Ibid.
230. Ibid., 201.
231. Ibid., 203.
232. Ibid., 205.
233. Ibid., 223.
234. Ibid., 232.
235. Ibid., 231.
236. Ibid., 234.

237. Ibid.
238. Ibid., 237.
239. Ibid., 245.
240. Ibid., 246.
241. Ibid., 244.
242. Ibid., 269.
243. Ibid., 270.
244. Ibid., 305.
245. Ibid., 307.
246. Ibid., 359.
247. Ibid., 277.
248. Ibid., 248.
249. Ibid.
250. Ibid., 301.

Bibliography

AccessWDUN. "New Holland United Methodist to Hold Final Service Sunday, Closing May Not Be Permanent." Last modified November 26, 2013. https://accesswdun.com.

Aladdin Company of Bay City. Central Michigan University. Last modified 2001. https://www.cmich.edu.

Andy Irvine Lyrics. "Aragon Mills." Last modified November 24, 2016. https://andyirvinelyrics.wordpress.com.

"Aragon Historical Society." Facebook. https://www.facebook.com.

Atlanta Constitution (Rome). "AllGood Shot Dead: By Dr. J.B.S. Holmes, His Brother-in-Law." January 21, 1890, 1.

——. "14 Are Arrested at Shannon Mill: Troopers Bring Prisoners to Atlanta." September 26, 1934, 3.

——. "Scenes of Unforgettable Horror Found in Ruin that Was Gainesville." April 7, 1936, 16.

——. "The Summerville Cotton Mills Are a Place Where Success Has Been Spelled in One Word—Co-Operation." July 22, 1917, 6.

Atlanta Journal. "Man Who 'Broke' News of Tragedy Tells His Story." April 7, 1936, 14.

Baker, J.S. *The Chattahoochee Boys*. Scotts Valley, CA: Createspace Independent Publishing, 2011.

Baker, Robert S. *Chattooga: The Story of a County and Its People*. Roswell, GA: W.H. Wolfe Associates, 1988.

Baker, Vera. "Mill Workers Oral Histories (MC 109)." Columbus State University Archives. Last modified February 12, 1988. https://archives. columbusstate.edu.

Bates, Ashley. "Weaving Tales." *Gainesville Times*. Last modified December 12, 2008. https://www.gainesvilletimes.com.

————. "Weaving Tales: Once the Home of a Cotton Mill, the Gainesville Mill Now Holds Tall Tales and More." *Gainesville Times*. Last modified December 12, 2008.

Battey, George M. *A History of Rome and Floyd County, State of Georgia, United States of America: Including Numerous Incidents of More than Local Interest, 1540–1922*. Atlanta, GA: Web and Vary Company, 1922.

Bellis, Mary. "Learn More About Textile Machinery Inventions." ThoughtCo. Last modified August 19, 2016. https://www.thoughtco. com.

Belmont–Mount Holly Banner News. "Remember the Rolling Snack Wagon?" http://banner-news.com.

Bostwick, Heather S. "Take Me Out to the Ballgame: The Northwest Georgia Textile League." Master's thesis, University of West Georgia, 2003.

Bowen, Andy. "Education Is a Gut Issue for Harris." *Marietta Daily Journal*, May 27, 1988, 25.

Brattain, Michelle. "'Labor's Best Friend': Talmadge, Paternalism, and the 1934 Strike." In *The Politics of Whiteness: Race, Workers, and Culture in the Modern South*. Athens: University of Georgia Press, 2004.

The Bricks Roswell. Last modified 2006. http://www.thebricksroswell.com.

A Brief History of Trion: Our Own Favored Land. Trion, GA: Espy Publishing Company Inc., 1976.

Brookshire, Vernon. "Echota Most Modern of Its Kind (in 1909)." *Past Times News Publishing*, August 2008, 37.

Brumbelow, Wesley. "Mill Workers Oral Histories (MC 109)." Columbus State University Archives. Last modified February 13, 1988. https:// archives.columbusstate.edu.

Bryson, Grady Jack. Interviewed by Sandy Moore of the Bartow History Museum.

Cain, Edna E. "Cotton Mills of the South: The Record of the Trion Cotton Mills Recalled. How the Venture Originated Successful in Manufacturing and in Marketing. Furnishing a Strong Object Lesson Miss Edna Cain Tells the Complete Story of the Trion Cotton Mills and Its Enterprising Men." *Atlanta Constitution*, April 10, 1898.

Calhoun Times. "Chattooga." Last modified August 2004. https://news.google.com.

———. "Polk County." September 1, 2004, 68, 78.

———. "Rockmart." September 1, 2004, 102.

———. September 20, 1934.

———. "Strike." September 17, 1934.

Carlton, David L. "Textile Industry." South Carolina Encyclopedia. Last modified May 22, 2018. http://www.scencyclopedia.org.

Carroll Free Press. "Georgia Weekly Press Association Party Visits Ideal Cotton Mill at Atco." September 14, 1911.

Castle, Sheri. "A Nab Is a Nab Is a Nab." Southern Foodways Alliance. Last modified December 19, 2017. https://www.southernfoodways.org.

Caudle, Alice, millworker. "Industrial Lore." American Life Histories: Manuscripts from the Federal Writers' Project, 1936–1940. Library of Congress. Last modified 1938. https://www.loc.gov.

Cauley, H.M. "Our Town: Canton Mills Influence Still Felt in North Metro Town." *Atlanta Journal and Constitution*, August 23, 2013. https://www.ajc.com.

The Center for Public History at the University of West Georgia. *The West Georgia Textile Heritage Trail.* Charleston, SC: Arcadia Publishing, 2015.

Child Labor Bulletin 2. Washington, D.C.: National Child Labor Committee, 1914, 1917.

Child Labor in the American South, Lewis Hine Collection, University of Maryland. "Georgia: Walker County Hosiery Mills." Last modified spring of 2007. https://userpages.umbc.edu.

City of Atlanta. "Documents for Historic Preservation of Atlanta, GA: Whittier Mill." Last modified October 28, 1994. https://www.atlantaga.gov.

City of Austell, Georgia. "Threadmill Complex History." Last modified 2018. https://www.austellga.gov.

Coats and Clark 200th Anniversary History Museum. Last modified 2019. http://www.coatsandclark200years.com.

Cobb Memorial Archives. "From Dope Wagons to Vending Machines." Last modified February 21, 2017. https://cobbmemorialarchives.wordpress.com.

Coleman, Billie. *Central Georgia Textile Mills.* Charleston, SC: Arcadia Publishing, 2017.

Colorado Historic Newspapers Collection. "Losses in Gainesville Tornado." Last modified June 5, 1903. https://www.coloradohistoricnewspapers.org.

Cooksey, Elizabeth B. "Chattooga County." Georgia Encyclopedia. Last modified September 12, 2018. https://www.georgiaencyclopedia.org.

Cooper, Alice A. Letter to family member about Sherman. Cooper Family Papers, 1912. Available at the Hargrett Archives, University of Georgia.

Crawford, Margaret. *Building the Workingman's Paradise: The Design of American Company Towns.* Brooklyn, NY: Verso, 1995.

Creative Home. "EverStrand Carpet, Carpeting Made from Recycled Bottles." Last modified September 26, 2014. http://creativehome. mohawkflooring.com.

Cunningham, Carolyn. "Cobb County's Old Clarkdale Park to Receive New Community Center." *Atlanta Journal Constitution.* Last modified April 12, 2019. https://www.ajc.com.

Cunyus, Lucy J. "Manufactures." In *The History of Bartow County: Formerly Cass.* 5th ed. Greenville, GA: Southern Historical Press, 1933.

Daly, Alexander. *Testimony of H.P. Meikleham.* Atlanta, GA: U.S. Commission on Industrial Relations, 1914. https://exhibit-archive.library.gatech.edu.

Deaton, Thomas, Myra Owens, Brenda Ownbey, Tammy Poplin and Vanessa Rinkel. *Dalton.* Charleston, SC: Arcadia Press, 2008.

Douthat, Strat. "Headache Powder: For What Ails You." *Los Angeles Times.* Last modified March 11, 2019. https://www.latimes.com.

Dufresne, Katherine. "Georgia: Rome Hosiery Mill." Child Labor in the American South, Lewis Hine Collection, University of Maryland. Last modified spring of 2007. https://userpages.umbc.edu.

Elachee Nature Science Center. "History of the Chicopee Woods." Last modified July 8, 2011. https://elacheenature.wordpress.com.

Engler, Lindsey. "Georgia: Massachusetts Mill, Lindale, Georgia." University of Maryland. Last modified 2007. https://userpages.umbc.edu.

Etowah Valley Historical Society. "Atco School." Last modified 2019. https://evhsonline.org.

"Exposition Cotton Mills Photographs." Atlanta History Center, Digital Resources of the Kenan Resource Center. http://album. atlantahistorycenter.com.

Fantinato, Nick. "Georgia: Walker County Hosiery Mills." University of Maryland. Last modified 2007. https://userpages.umbc.edu.

Federal Writers' Project. *The WPA Guide to Georgia: The Peach State.* San Antonio, TX: Trinity University Press, 1939.

Fink, Gary M. *The Fulton Bag and Cotton Mills Strike of 1914–1915: Espionage, Labor Conflict, and New South Industrial Relations.* Ithaca, NY: Cornell University Press, 1993.

Flamming, Douglas. *Creating the Modern South: Millhands and Managers in Dalton, Georgia, 1884–1984.* Chapel Hill: University of North Carolina Press, 2000.

Gable, Jeff. "Anchor Duck Monument to Be Unveiled Saturday; Annual Reunion to Be Sept. 26." *Northwest Georgia News.* Last modified September 16, 2009. http://www.northwestgeorgianews.com.

Gainesville News. February 3, 1904.

———. June 3, 1903.

———. May 18, 1904.

———. November 5, 1902.

Gainesville Times. "Gainesville Mill: Cotton Mill Purchased in 1901, Started in South Carolina." https://www.gainesvilletimes.com.

———. "Times Parent Company Buys Historic Gainesville Mill." Last modified July 19, 2016. https://www.gainesvilletimes.com.

Garner, John. *The Company Town: Architecture and Society in the Early Industrial Age.* New York: Oxford University Press, 1992. Kindle ed.

GenDisasters. "Gainesville, GA Tornado, Jun 1903." http://www.gendisasters.com.

Georgia Cracker (Gainesville). "Come Down and See." February 2, 1901.

———. "Dr. J.H. Downey of Pacolet comes to New Holland." October 19, 1901.

———. Image 1. March 17, 1900. Georgia Historic Newspapers. https://gahistoricnewspapers.galileo.usg.edu.

———. Image 7, "Gainesville Vesta Mills." January 26, 1901.

———. October 19, 1901.

———. "What She Wants, She Gets." February 2, 1901.

Georgia Historic Newspapers. https://gahistoricnewspapers.galileo.usg.edu.

Georgia State University Library Research Guides. "Southern Labor Archives: Work N' Progress—Lessons and Stories: Part III: The Southern Textile Industry." Last modified May 29, 2019. http://research.library.gsu.edu.

Gibbons, Beth. Personal interview. Georgia Northwestern Technical College, February 5, 2019.

Gill, Jeff. "Chicopee Once a Thriving Mill Community." *Gainesville Times.* Last modified December 27, 2012. https://www.gainesvilletimes.com.

———. "New Holland a New Village Rising." *Gainesville Times.* Last modified March 16, 2014. https://www.gainesvilletimes.com.

Grady, Henry W. "The New South." In *Henry W. Grady and His Speeches.* Atlanta, GA: Chas. P. Byrd, 1895. https://dlg.galileo.usg.edu.

Gray, Greg. "The Cedartown Cotton Company and Charles Adamson from the Polk County History Book Submitted by Greg Gray Search." GA American History and Genealogy Project. Last modified September 11, 2018.

Green, Hardy. *The Company Town: The Industrial Edens and Satanic Mills that Shaped the American Economy.* N.p.: Basic Books, 2012. This book by Hardy Green does a survey of American Company Towns.

Gudger, J.B. "Chattanooga Tennessee: 'The Industrial Center of the South.'" *Chattanooga Times*, 1885.

———. "Dalton, the Chief City of the North Georgia Tier of Counties." *Chattanooga Times*, 1885.

Gurowitz, Margaret. "Chicopee Village." Kilmer House. Last modified May 22, 2013. http://www.kilmerhouse.com.

Hall, Jacquelyn D., James L. Leloudis, Robert R. Korstad and Mary Murphy. *Like a Family: The Making of a Southern Cotton Mill World.* 2nd ed. Chapel Hill: University of North Carolina Press, 2012.

Hannah, Sallie Kate, and George Stoney. "Sallie Kate Hannah Interview." 1990. The Uprising of '34 Collection, Special Collections and Archives, Georgia State University. http://digitalcollections.library.gsu.edu.

Hayes, Brad. "The Night General Sherman Stayed in Trion." Facebook. Last modified February 13, 2013. https://www.facebook.com.

Hayes, Donald M. Personal interview. Calhoun, Georgia, June 3, 2019.

Hedley, Fenwick Y. *Marching through Georgia. Pen-Pictures of Every-Day Life in General Sherman's Army, from the Beginning of the Atlanta Campaign Until the Close of the War, by F.Y. Hedley.* Illustrated by F.L. Stoddard. N.p., 1890.

Hicks, Joseph Wilson. *Family History of Joseph Wilson Hicks.* Lindale, GA, n.d.

Hill, Jodie Leon, and Thomas A. Scott. "KSU Oral History Series, No. 80." Interview with J.B. Tate. Last modified 2008. https://dlg.usg.edu.

Irvine, Andy. "Industrial Lore." American Life Histories: Manuscripts from the Federal Writers' Project, 1936–1940. Library of Congress. Last modified 2014. https://www.loc.gov.

Jackson, M.L. "Baldy." *Lindale: One of the Best Mill Towns in the Southland, the Home of 5,000 Contented People.* Lindale, GA: Massachusetts Cotton Mills—A Division of Pepperell Manufacturing Company, 1939.

Johnson & Johnson—Our Story. "Building Chicopee Mill and Village." https://ourstory.jnj.com.

Johnson, Lee. "Gainesville Mill: Cotton Mill Purchased in 1901, Started in South Carolina." *Gainesville Times.* Last modified December 22, 2012. https://www.gainesvilletimes.com.

Johnston, Rebecca. *Canton*. Charleston, SC: Arcadia Publishing, 2015.

Jones, Robert T. "The Cotton Mill Situation: Mr. R.T. Jones, President of the Canton Cotton Mills and the Bank of Canton, Writes a Logical and Sensible Article of the Present Situation of Southern Cotton Mills." *Cherokee Advance (Canton)*, December 25, 1903.

The Journal. Whitfield-Murray Historical Society Newsletter. Dalton, GA, 2019.

Kantrowitz, Marc. *Canton*. Charleston, SC: Arcadia Publishing, 2000.

Kidd, Wanda. Personal interview. Calhoun, Georgia, May 20, 2019.

Kilmer House—Johnson & Johnson. Last modified 2019. http://www.kilmerhouse.com.

King, Savannah. "New Holland: Mill Brought Life, Closeness to Small Village." *Gainesville Times*. Last modified December 23, 2012. https://www.gainesvilletimes.com.

KnowItAll. "When the Mill Closes Down." N.d. https://www.knowitall.org.

Kuhn, Clifford M. *Contesting the New South Order: The 1914–1915 Strike at Atlanta's Fulton Mills*. Chapel Hill: University of North Carolina Press, 2003.

———. *Living Atlanta: An Oral History of the City, 1914–1948*. Athens: University of Georgia Press, 2005.

Lat34North. "Clarkdale Historic District c. 1931." http://lat34north.com.

Lee, John K. "The Story of Asaph Perry." Cherokee County Digital History Project. Last modified 2003. http://www.dhpp.org/Cherokee/narrative/canton_cotton.htm.

Leland, Elizabeth. "Sip of Relief." *Our State Magazine*. Last modified May 30, 2012. https://www.ourstate.com.

Lindale Mill Filming. "The Mill." http://lindalemill.com.

Lindale Year Book. Lindale, GA, 1939.

Longworth, April. "Behind the Strike: How Atlanta Responded to the Investigation of the Fulton Bag and Cotton Mill." *Armstrong Undergraduate Journal of History* 1, no. 2 (April 2011).

Lorence, James J. "The Workers of Chicopee: Progressive Paternalism and the Culture of Accommodation in a Modern Mill Village." *Georgia Historical Quarterly* 91, no. 3 (2007): 292.

Manthorne, Jason. "Greensboro." New Georgia Encyclopedia. Last modified July 17, 2018. https://www.georgiaencyclopedia.org.

Marbury, J.B. *U.S. Weather Bureau Monthly Weather Review June 1903: Tornado at Gainesville, Georgia*. Atlanta, GA: U.S. Weather Bureau, 1903.

Marietta Daily Journal. "Former Threadmill Workers Spin Yarns at Reunion." Last modified October 5, 2014. https://www.mdjonline.com.

————. "What's the Difference between Acworth and Clarkdale Thread Mills?" November 18, 1954.

Martin, Clarece. "The Mill Women and Children of Roswell, Uprooted: In 1947, Synthia Catherine Stewart Boyd Recalled How Union Army Captured, Shipped Away Mill Workers." *Atlanta Journal Constitution*, January 7, 1999.

Mastrianni, Keia. "Eatymology: Coke and Peanuts." The Local Palate. Last modified February 13, 2018. https://thelocalpalate.com.

McCanless, E.A. *The Story of a Man, a Town and a Mill*. N.p., 1949.

McCollum, Greg. *Chattooga County*. Images of America Series. Charleston, SC: Arcadia Publishing, 2012.

McGill, Eula, and Jacquelyn Hall. "Oral History Interview with Eula McGill, February 3, 1976." Interview G-0040-1." Documenting the American South: Oral Histories of the American South. Southern Oral History Program Collection, Southern Historical Collection, Wilson Library, University of North Carolina–Chapel Hill. Last modified February 3, 1976. https://docsouth.unc.edu.

Middle Tennessee State University. "Celanese Mill Village: Harwell Family." 1942. http://digital.mtsu.edu.

————. "Celanese Village." Digital Collections, Digital Scholarship Initiatives. http://cdm15838.contentdm.oclc.org.

Mill News 22, no. 16. "Lafayette Cotton Mills" (1920): 82.

The Mill on Etowah. "Canton, Georgia." Last modified 2019. http://etowahmill.com.

Montgomery, Wynn. "Georgia's 1948 Phenoms and the Bonus Rule." Society for American Baseball Research. Last modified 2010. https://sabr.org.

Mosely, Beulah S. "Anchor Duck Mills." *Womans' Magazine* 2, no. 11 (March 15, 1908).

Mount Vernon Mills Inc. "Denim." http://www.mvmdenim.com.

Murray, Bill. "Pictures of the Past: Mill Leaguers Played for Nothing but Love of the Game." *Gainesville Times*. Last modified June 25, 2008. https://www.gainesvilletimes.com.

Myrick, Kevin. "Former Workers Reminisce with Shannon Mill Family at Reunion." *Northwest Georgia News*. Last modified September 20, 2009. http://www.northwestgeorgianews.com.

National Child Labor Committee. *Child Labor Bulletin* 2. New York: self-published, 1914.

————. *Child Labor in Georgia*. Pamphlets. New York: Macmillan, 1910.

National Child Labor Committee and Owen R. Lovejoy. *Child Labor in 1912: With Special Articles on Child Workers in New York Tenements; Children on the Stage.* National Child Labor Committee, 1912.

National Child Labor Committee Collection. "Arrangement and Access." Library of Congress. Last modified 1912. https://www.loc.gov.

———. "Background and Scope." Library of Congress. https://www.loc.gov.

New Georgia Encyclopedia. "Cotton Mill Worker." Library of Congress. https://www.georgiaencyclopedia.org.

———. "Crown Cotton Mill." Library of Congress. https://www.georgiaencyclopedia.org.

The 1936 Downtown Gainesville Tornado Walk. Flyer. Gainesville, GA: City of Gainesville, n.d. https://www.gainesville.org.

"The 1936 Gainesville Tornado: Effects of the Tornado on Industry." Digital Library of Georgia. Last modified June 30, 2008. http://dlg.galileo.usg.edu.

Northwest Georgia News. "Polk's Past Mills Provide Tourism Opportunities." Last modified May 13, 2014. http://www.northwestgeorgianews.com.

Oliver, Charles. "The Mill Offers Something Different for Dalton in Shopping." *Daily Citizen.* Last modified April 2, 2018. https://www.dailycitizen.news.

Original Poems and Family History Blog | Formerly Taylor Family Poems and Family History Writings. "First Baptist Church Summerville Georgia." Last modified 2014. https://taylorfamilypoems.wordpress.com.

Past Times News Publishing Company (Rome). "Anchor Duck: Nothing Is Now Left of the Mill that Dominated South Rome." August 2008.

———. "Chattooga County." August 2004.

Petite, Mary D. *The Women Will Howl: The Union Army Capture of Roswell and New Manchester, Georgia, and the Forced Relocation of Mill Workers.* Jefferson, NC: McFarland & Company, 2010.

Pfohl, Bailey. "Edward Kemble." Norman Rockwell Museum. https://www.illustrationhistory.org.

Popham, Eleanor H. Interview. December 2018.

Pritchett, Elizabeth. Interviewed by Judith Helfand, n.d. L1995-13_AV0777. The Uprising of '34 Collection, Special Collections and Archives, Georgia State University. http://digitalcollections.library.gsu.edu.

Proctor, Aungelique. "Douglas County Was Created Originally to Honor Frederick Douglass." WAGA Fox. Last modified March 1, 2017. http://www.fox5atlanta.com.

Ragland, Mike. "Guest Column: History of Rome's Anchor Duck." *Northwest Georgia News*. Last modified June 9, 2017. http://www. northwestgeorgianews.com.

———. "Guest Column: Rome Hosiery Mill Once Led Nation." *Northwest Georgia News*. Last modified February 4, 2012. http://www. northwestgeorgianews.com.

Rawlings, William J. "The Myth of the Boll Weevil." *Georgia Backroads* (Spring 2014).

Reddy, Frank. "From the Start, Chicopee Was a Cut Above." *Gainesville Times*. Last modified June 15, 2015. https://www.gainesvilletimes.com.

Rock Barn Cherokee Historical Society. "Canton Cotton Mill #2." www. rockbarn.org.

Rockmart History Museum. "Historic Rockmart." https:// rockmarthistorymuseum.com.

Rossner, Angie, and George Story. August 14, 1990. The Uprising of '34 Collection, Special Collections and Archives, Georgia State University. http://digitalcollections.library.gsu.edu.

Roswell Women. "Roswell Civil War." Last modified 2018. https://www. roswellwomen.com.

Russell, Lisa M. *Lost Towns of North Georgia*. Charleston, SC: The History Press, 2016. This book has three chapters dedicated to mill towns, mine towns and company towns.

———. *Underwater Ghost Towns of North Georgia*. Charleston, SC: The History Press, 2018.

Rylands, Traci. "The Long Walk Home: The Story of Adeline Bagley Buice." Adventures in Cemetery Hopping. Last modified October 27, 2018. https://adventuresincemeteryhopping.com.

Shaw, Barton C. "*The New South* by Henry W. Grady." *Atlanta Historical Society* (Summer 1886): 55–62.

Shores, Heather S. "Working to Play, Playing to Work: The Northwest Georgia Textile League." Society for American Baseball Research. Last modified 2010. https://sabr.org.

Simpson, Lydia. "All Roads Lead: From Ancient Silk Road to Multinational Synthetic Fibers Industry in a Southern Appalachian Town." PhD dissertation, Middle Tennessee State University, 2017.

———. "In Progress: Celanese Digital Collection." Walker Library, Middle Tennessee State University. https://lydiasimpson.carbonmade.com.

Sloop, Terry. "Rudy York." Society for American Baseball Research. https:// sabr.org.

Storey, Steve. "Streetcars in Gainesville." Georgia's Railroad History and Heritage. https://railga.com.

Straus, Matevz, and Razvan Zamfira. *The Re-Birth of the Company Town: How Corporations Are Reshaping Life, Work and Play in the City.* Scotts Valley: Createspace Independent Publishing Platform, 2016. Kindle ed.

Sullivan, Buddy. *Georgia: A State History.* Charleston: Arcadia Publishing, 2010.

Tetiyevsky, Charlie. "Dope Wagons and the Road to Cocaine-Free Coca-Cola." PRØHBTD. Last modified May 1, 2017. https://prohbtd.com.

Trimble, Stanley W. "Soil Erosion." New Georgia Encyclopedia. Last modified July 26, 2017. https://www.georgiaencyclopedia.org.

Trion Facts. Last modified February 13, 2013.

University of Maryland. "Child Labor in the American South." Last modified 2007. https://userpages.umbc.edu.

The Uprising of '34. Directed by George C. Stoney and Judith Hefland. Documentary Educational Resources. DVD. 1995.

U.S. Commission on Industrial Relations. "Unpublished Records of the Division of Research and Investigation: Reports, Staff Studies, and Background Research Materials." 1985.

Vardeman, Johnny. "Clubhouse from Chicopee Filled with Memories." *Gainesville Times.* Last modified November 4, 2018. https://www.gainesvilletimes.com.

———. "MilliKids Kept Plenty Busy in Mill Village Life." *Gainesville Times.* Last modified February 3, 2013. https://www.gainesvilletimes.com.

———. "New Holland Was a Milestone in Hall County History." *Gainesville Times.* Last modified November 22, 2009. https://www.gainesvilletimes.com.

Vardeman, Johnny, and Kit Dunlap. "Hall Tales, Episode 2: Industry, from Way Back when to Now." *Gainesville Times.* Last modified July 27, 2018. https://www.gainesvilletimes.com.

Vardeman, Johnny, Kay Scoville and Dale Jaeger. "Hall Tales, Episode 7: Chicopee Village (Audio)." *Gainesville Times.* Last modified October 12, 2018. https://www.gainesvilletimes.com.

Varrassi, John. "Transforming the Textile Industry." American Society of Mechanical Engineers. Last modified April 2012. https://www.asme.org.

Waffle, Alan, Yvonnie Hill, Ruth Archer, George Stoney, Judith Helfand and Jamie Stoney. "Alan Waffle, Yvonnie Hill and Ruth Archer Interview." 1995. The Uprising of '34 Collection, Special Collections and Archives, Georgia State University. http://digitalcollections.library.gsu.edu.

Wagner, Michael A., and Cherokee County Society. *Canton Cotton Mills: A Pictorial History.* N.p., 2014.

Walker, Doug. "Celanese Mill and Village Being Pitched for National Register of Historic Places." *Rome News-Tribune.* Last modified October 5, 2018. www.northwestgeorgianews.com.

———. "Shannon Mill: Salvaging a Piece of History." *Northwest Georgia News (Rome)*, August 11, 2011.

The Watters District Council for Historic Preservation. "Brighton Employees Buying War Bonds." https://www.wattersdistrictcouncil.org.

———. "Modern Medical Clinic Established in Shannon." https://www.wattersdistrictcouncil.org.

———. "Watters District Council." Last modified 2019. https://www.wattersdistrictcouncil.org.

———. "Watters." Last modified December 1947. https://www.wattersdistrictcouncil.org.

Waymarking. "Trion Factory Cotton Mile Marker." Last modified October 12, 2008. www.waymarking.com.

West Georgia Textile Heritage Trail. "Aragon." Last modified 2019. http://westgatextiletrail.com.

———. "Berryton." http://westgatextiletrail.com.

———. "Calhoun." Last modified 2019. http://westgatextiletrail.com.

———. "Cedartown." http://westgatextiletrail.com.

———. "Douglasville." Last modified 2018. http://westgatextiletrail.com.

———. "Lafayette." Last modified 2019. http://westgatextiletrail.com.

———. "Rockmart." Last modified 2019. http://westgatextiletrail.com.

———. "Rome." http://westgatextiletrail.com.

———. "Rossville." Last modified 2019. http://westgatextiletrail.com.

———. "Summerville." http://westgatextiletrail.com.

———. "Trion." http://westgatextiletrail.com.

———. "Tufts of the Past: Dalton Whitfield Self-Guided Tour." http://westgatextiletrail.com.

Wickersham, Mary E., and Robert P. Yehl. "The Cotton Mill Village Turned City." *Journal of Urban History* 40, no. 5 (2014): 917–32.

Wilder, Kristina. "Pepperell Students Preserving Stories of Mill Town." *Northwest Georgia News.* Last modified March 27, 2017. https://www.northwestgeorgianews.com.

Willis, J. Archie. "A Cotton Mill Whose Idea of Welfare Work Is to Place Its Operatives on an Independent Basis; Where the Georgia Moonshiner Is Transformed into a Law-Abiding Citizen; and Where the Children Are

Given the Advantages of Compulsory Education." *Atlanta Journal*, March 4, 1917.

Wing Foot Clan. "Another Promotion of Interest to Goodyearites Is that of Former Private Lawrence Collins of Camp Bowie, Texas, Who Has Been Elevated to the Corporal of a Tank Unit. Lawrence Is the Son of Mr. Ben Collins of the Carding Department." May 8, 1942.

———. "Billion-a-Month for Victory." May 8, 1942.

———. "Emma Gillespie Is Atco's Largest Girl." December 20, 1929.

———. "James W. Brown, Brother of Mrs. Hoyt Green, Became the First Bartow County Man to Be Lost in the Service of His Country in World War II." May 8, 1942.

Wright, Barry. "Meikleham." Presentation, Lindale Bible Class, Lindale, Georgia, August 1, 1937.

Wright, Henry G. "Mill Workers' Oral Histories Swift Spinning Mill." Interview by Fred Stearns. Columbus State University. Last modified February 22, 1988. https://archives.columbusstate.edu.

INDEX

Roosevelt, Franklin Delano 111, 158, 159, 187

S

Sherman, William Tecumseh 21, 71, 72, 77, 94, 95, 99
stretch-out 25, 49, 78, 139, 159, 160, 187, 192
strikes 18, 26, 27, 28, 49, 54, 62, 68, 71, 77, 78, 79, 81, 86, 96, 98, 102, 123, 124, 134, 139, 158, 159, 160, 164, 165, 168, 187, 188

T

textile mill era 17, 49
Tubize 125

U

unions 18, 25, 26, 27, 42, 49, 77, 79, 98, 124, 134, 138, 139, 159, 161, 168, 187, 188, 189, 191, 192
U.S. Bureau of Labor 36
U.S. Commission on Industrial Relations 101, 102

V

Vesta Mills 151, 152

W

Wingfoot Clan 60, 62
World War II 17, 40, 48, 60, 62, 70, 80, 113, 118, 124, 125, 168, 188

Y

Yorkship Village 9, 10

About the Author

Lisa M. Russell supports regional historical and archaeology societies. She has been on several Georgia Public Broadcasting (GPB) documentaries and podcasts. Russell was enlisted by producers for Discovery Channel's *Expedition X: Lake Lanier*. She earned her Master of Arts degree in professional writing from Kennesaw State University. Lisa teaches English full time at Georgia Northwestern Technical College. She is a part-time professor of communication at Kennesaw State University and writing in Reinhardt University's MFA program. In her "spare time," you can find Lisa exploring North Georgia for her next story.

Visit us at
www.historypress.com
···